THE WORD
IN AND OUT OF SEASON

Homilies for the Sundays
of Advent and Lent

by Richard Viladesau

Paulist Press
New York and Mahwah, N.J.

also by Richard Viladesau
published by Paulist Press

THE WORD IN AND OUT OF SEASON, CYCLE A
THE WORD IN AND OUT OF SEASON, CYCLE B
THE WORD IN AND OUT OF SEASON, CYCLE C

Copyright © 1996
by Richard Viladesau

Library of Congress Cataloging-in-Publication Data

Viladesau, Richard.
    Homilies for the Sundays of Advent and Lent / by Richard Viladesau.
        p.   cm. —(The Word in and out of season ; [v. 4])
        Includes bibliographical references.
        ISBN 0-8091-3626-0 (alk. paper)
        1. Advent sermons.   2. Lenten sermons.   3. Catholic Church—Sermons.   4. Church year sermons.   5. Sermons, American.
        I. Title.   II. Series: Viladesau, Richard. Word in and out of season ; v. 4.
    BX1756.V63W67 vol. 4
    252'.6 s—dc20
    [252'.61]   95-31979
                                                                                    CIP

Published by Paulist Press
997 Macarthur Boulevard
Mahwah, New Jersey 07430

Printed and bound in the
United States of America

Table of Contents

*To My Classmates
on the 25th Anniversary of Our Ordination—
Ad Multos Annos*

Introduction

Preaching in the Seasons of Anticipation and Preparation

In a certain local parish, the Rosary Society sponsors an annual St. Patrick's Day dance. This year, in order to get the band they wanted, the ladies were forced to hold the event a full two weeks before the feast. The only day available was a Friday: a Friday in Lent, one of the few remaining days of abstinence in the calendar. No one, including the pastor of the parish, felt the slightest hesitation in attending and feasting at the celebration—or in celebrating again, two weeks later, when the feast itself occurred on another Lenten Friday. In the same parish—and in many others—because of people's work schedules, there are several big Christmas parties held in the middle of Advent. And because of spring recess, the children in the parochial school celebrate Easter in their classrooms before the Triduum.

None of these examples is unusual. But they all point to a particular liturgical problem in the contemporary church. The cycle of "seasons" associated with the church's major feasts is perhaps the most salient feature of the Christian liturgical year. At one time it formed the unquestionably accepted framework for Christians' lives. Yet the meaning of those seasons, once taken so much for granted, has become increasingly marginal to many people, including those closest to the church. For this reason the liturgical seasons offer to the preacher special difficulties—and, perhaps, special opportunities. Before dealing with the specific nature of the preparatory seasons covered in this book, therefore, it is fitting to look briefly into the idea of "seasons"; to inquire how they relate to the Christian view of time; to explore their connection with the "ordinary" and primary liturgical celebration, the Sunday eucharist; and to examine the nature of the difficulties and opportunities they afford.

The Church "Seasons" and the Christian Idea of Time

The very fact of the division of the church year is significant. Although we take for granted the recurrence of a cycle of feasts and seasons, and experience a certain immediate meaningfulness in their celebration, the theological justification of this aspect of the Christian liturgy is not self-evident.

Indeed, at first glance there might seem to be a tension between the cyclical nature of the liturgical year and the view of time implied by the Christian conception of salvation history.

As the well-known studies of Mircea Eliade have pointed out,[1] a cyclical world-view is typical of the Oriental and the ancient pre-Christian religions, insofar as they either consist in or subsume within themselves the worship of the forces of nature. The "myth of the eternal return" is the religious articulation of the rhythm of vegetative life, seen as the paradigm of the mystery of the world. The periodic renewal of the world is symbolized by gods who die and return to life: "the cosmic cycle is conceived as the indefinite repetition of the same rhythm: birth, death, rebirth."[2] Humans mystically join in this cycle, and in some way cause its renewal, by its ritual reenactment each year. The cyclical view of time is sometimes joined, in the great Indic religions, with a view of this world as illusory and/or lacking in substance, so that historical existence is devalued.[3]

The contemporary secular view of time, on the other hand, is related to the objectifying mentality of modern technology. Although the scientific notion of time has undergone reformulation under the influence of Einsteinian relativity and is opened to further questions by the ongoing discoveries of quantum physics,[4] our "common sense" view of time remains that of the Newtonian universe: the world of clocks, measuring equally spaced, universal, objective time.[5] This time is neutral and democratic. Subjectively, time goes slowly when we are bored and quickly when we're having fun; but "objective" time knows no such differentiations: it flows at an equal pace for all. It is measured not by human perception, feeling, or projects, but by the relation of things to other things: ultimately, the relation of mechanical instruments to the motion of the planet. This is the time of the workplace and of technology; it gives us a framework that permits exact measurements and comparisons that are independent of subjective factors. This time is also "cyclical," in the sense that the physical phenomena that are its measure—the planet's daily rotation on its axis and yearly revolution around the sun—are repetitive, at least within the short run of human existence on earth.

The Judeo-Christian idea of time, while not denying the validity of "secular" time, has a different center of interest. It sees time in relation to human life and its goal. As Walter Kasper notes, "The first characteristic of the biblical view of time is that it does not regard time as purely quantitative. It is not a continuous and homogeneous sequence of days and hours, but qualitative. Time is measured by its content; it depends what it is time for. 'For everything there is a season, and a time for every matter under heaven.'"[6]

Unlike the mythic cyclical view, on the other hand, the Judeo-Christian theological view conceives time as linear and eschatological.[7] Time is God's creation; it has a beginning and an end. The "end" of time, moreover, is not simply the cessation of its flow, but is a goal that will be reached.[8] History—

the course of human time in the world—has a direction and a purpose. It is the field of action for the accomplishment of God's creative and salvific design. As such, it is the condition for free activity and for the development of human relationships, which are the means for the accomplishment of God's will: the sharing of God's life with creation. Within this directed flow of time, there is the possibility of irrepeatable and eternally significant events of personal self-disposition toward God. Time is thus the locus of salvation history.

What is specifically Christian in this notion of time is the conviction that the eschatological goal of salvation history—in biblical language, God's "Kingdom," or loving rule over creation—has appeared definitively within the world. Christ is seen as the unique mediator of this event;[9] in him, something has happened once for all. Nevertheless, the history of salvation continues: what has "already" occurred in Christ, especially in the proleptic event of the resurrection, anticipates a future completion and calls for a present response. For this reason, the New Testament frequently speaks of the time initiated by Christ as the καιρός (*kairos*)—the decisive time, the time of opportunity (see for example Jn 7:6, 8; Rom 5:6, 13:11; Col 4:5, 6:10; Eph 5:16).[10]

This view of time and history determines the perspective of Christian liturgy. Its celebrations—including the "cycles" of feasts and seasons—are not the yearly repetition of a cosmic drama, as in mythological consciousness; they have rather the structure of commemoration—thankful remembrance of a distinct historical event that took place within the world: i.e., within the framework of that time which can also be measured in an "objective" and secular way, and is in this sense definitively "past."

Nevertheless, to say that this event has religious significance implies that its meaning is not confined to its own historical situation. It has an orientation to and effect on the future, not merely in the sense of those times that are subsequent to it, but in its absolute or "eschatological" sense: the end and fulfillment of time. From another point of view, one may also say that these events are effected precisely *by* the future—that is, by the final triumph of God's reign, which breaks into time in a definitive and revelatory way in Jesus' resurrection, giving a new meaning to his entire life and message.[11] Only by having this relationship to the absolute future can the Christ event possess an essential meaning (one that goes beyond the factual influence of the life and preaching of Jesus on the course of history) for our *present* relation to God and for our salvation.

It is this relationship of past event to future consummation that gives to Christian worship its distinctive characteristic: to be remembrance and, at the same time, the anticipation of the full and final accomplishment of what is remembered. The tension between these two elements allows us to experience our present as being encompassed in the power of God's already victorious salvific action while also being challenged by the ethical imperative to take a personal stance toward that action, to accept and effect it in our lives.

The Seasonal Cycle and the Sunday Liturgy

Although the commemorative and anticipatory structure of Christian worship is made present in each of the sacraments, it is the eucharist, and in particular the Sunday celebration of the universal church, that embodies in a preeminent way the mystery of salvation. In the words of the Second Vatican Council:

> . . . The other sacraments, and indeed all ecclesiastical ministries and works of the apostolate, are bound up with the Eucharist and are directed towards it. For in the

most blessed Eucharist is contained the whole spiritual good of the Church, namely Christ himself our Pasch and the living bread which gives life [to humanity] through his flesh—that flesh which is given life and gives life through the Holy Spirit. Thus [all] are invited and led to offer themselves, their works and all creation with Christ. For this reason the Eucharist appears as the source and summit of all preaching of the Gospel . . .[12]

The "ordinary" Sunday, then, is the church's original "feast day"[13] and Easter celebration.[14] This is in accord with the integral character of the salvific event. In each eucharist, the *whole* of the Christ event is made present and celebrated. But this means that there is a certain reduplication of meaning between the Sunday liturgy and the liturgical seasons:

Once each week, on the day which she has called the Lord's Day, the church keeps the memory of the Lord's resurrection. She also celebrates it once every year, together with his blessed passion at Easter, that most solemn of all feasts.

In the course of the year, moreover, she unfolds the whole mystery of Christ from the incarnation and nativity to the ascension, to Pentecost and the expectation of the blessed hope of the coming of the Lord.[15]

There is therefore a certain dialectic between the celebration of the whole (the "ordinary" Sunday liturgy) and of its elements (the seasons): through every "season," whatever its focus, it is the Sunday eucharist, containing and remembering the resurrection as the epitome of the whole salvific event, which is the central and original commemoration. The history of liturgy recounts the development of the "duplication" of the commemoration of the whole in the celebration of its parts. At first, the church did not celebrate "mysteries," but *the* mystery": the resurrection of Christ, commemorated every Sunday. Then was introduced the "great Sunday" of Easter, and (under the influence of Judaism) its prolongation in the feast of Pentecost.[16] Later, the other feasts and their seasons evolved. But these remain subordinate, theologically, to the central commemoration that takes place on each Sunday. We celebrate the "parts" only in the light of their completion; hence it can be said that the church celebrates only a single mystery, which pervades every church season.

Nevertheless, there is a valid psychological reason for the celebration of individual "mysteries" and the division of the church year into seasons. There are many diverse aspects of the single mystery of God's victorious self-gift to humanity in Christ, and of our relation to it. It is impossible for us to focus on all at once. Hence, it is legitimate and necessary for us, as a community, to emphasize one or another aspect at a time.[17] Moreover, although the resurrection is the culmination and completion of the Christ event, it is the whole life of Christ that it unifies, validates, and glorifies; therefore, the Easter celebration of the eucharist is related through the year to the principal events of Christ's earthly life and mission. "Through the yearly cycle the Church unfolds the entire mystery of Christ."[18]

Preaching in the Seasons: Two Difficulties

The celebration of the seasons presents two difficulties that particularly affect the preacher. The first is a theological one that underscores the conflict between the Christian and the mythological-religious cyclical concept of time. The second is a practical one that stems from the conflict between the Christian and the secular concept of time, particularly as lived in contemporary society.

The very nature of the "cycle" of seasons presents a danger of misunderstanding. There is a sense, of course, in which the liturgical year may be seen as "the dramatic retelling of Jesus' life and the salvation given to us."[19] But there is a popular tendency—frequently uncorrected or even encouraged by preachers—to look at the succession of seasons and their liturgical readings as though their purposes were historical or biographical, rather than theological. When this occurs, there is a danger of seeing the liturgical year as a cyclical repetition or renewal of the life of Christ, as in mythological consciousness. Then the specifically Christian "once-for-all" nature of the mystery of salvation is lost.

The celebration of the resurrection (which theologically includes the "giving" of the Spirit) is the "ordinary" and permanent context of Christian worship. It is the recognition and remembrance of the eschatological character of the Christ event: an already accomplished reality that makes God's final future victory present in us. Hence it is the *living* reality of the Spirit, producing the resurrected life in the community, that is the context for every liturgical celebration. When this is forgotten, there is a danger of losing the always-present character of salvation as God's gift, with its accompanying imperative. In that case, there is a corresponding danger that existential engagement could be replaced by a merely imaginative and affective spirituality: an emotional relation to the events of Jesus' earthly life, rather than an existential participation in the resurrected life, present in us.

Of course, imagination, affectivity, and drama all have a proper and indeed critical place in Christian spirituality and celebration; but if they are its exclusive content, they run the risk of becoming separated from both the reality of everyday life and the transcendental experience of grace. Liturgy then becomes indistinguishable from theater (as in primitive societies). Its purpose is reduced to a dramatic catharsis of religious emotion. The celebration of the yearly seasons becomes the aesthetic repetition of pious feelings and moral messages associated with stages in Christ's earthly existence. The "imitation of Christ" is focused on the reproduction of Jesus' reported or (more frequently) imagined attitudes and behavior, rather than on his paradigmatic relationship to God's presence through the same Spirit that animates our existence.

A different kind of difficulty arises from the conflict between the church's seasonal "times" and the secular experience of life. The liturgical year was formed by the context, habits, and mentality of a Christian community in an agriculturally based, pre-technological society. For the majority of people, life was determined by certain unchanging rhythms, which were more or less common to the entire community. Whether faith, in its theological meaning, was actually more common in the "Christendom" of the past than it is today is impossible to say; but certainly Christian religion was a much more explicit part of the social structure, and for many was a prominent feature of everyday life. The existence of sacred times and places was taken for granted. Within a sacred and hierarchical view of the universe, the biblical (and/or the mythological) sense of time was the framework not only for the church's liturgical life, but also for everyday existence.

The modern secular world-view, by contrast, is associated with the "democratic" and homogeneous view of time typical of science, the market and the workplace. In the urban context, even the seasons of nature make less difference than they did to our ancestors. Central heating and air conditioning allow us to live our indoor lives with minimal difference winter and summer. Refrigeration and the global market combine to provide fresh fruits and vegetables year round; our diets are no longer determined by seasonal foods.

Even more significantly, perhaps, many people's occupations are indifferent to seasonal change. Secular time, which forms the basic structure of Christians' everyday lives in a pluralistic society, is uniform, global, and unvarying.

Nevertheless, American secular society has feasts and "seasons" of its own, each with its own rituals and times of preparation. They are reinforced by advertising and the media, and by the scheduling of holidays from work and school around them. With many local variations, we observe such occasions as Labor Day, Halloween (which from a single day has now almost become a season, with ghostly decorations hanging for weeks in advance in shops and homes), Thanksgiving, the holiday shopping season, "the holidays" (Christmas, Hannukah, and New Year), spring break, St. Patrick's Day, Memorial Day, summer vacation. Parents are very aware of other kinds of seasons, centered on activities: soccer season, swimming season, baseball season, football season, etc.

Although these societal markers of time may sometimes complement the liturgical seasons,[20] they are more likely to be either irrelevant to or in conflict with them; and since the former are more pervasive, because tied to commerce and the media, they tend to overshadow the church's observances. Except perhaps in cloisters and monasteries, even those who try to live the liturgical seasons are living society's seasons as well, and frequently have to compromise.

A particular difficulty arises insofar as society has adopted and secularized once-Christian feasts, especially Christmas. The celebration of Advent as a season of spiritual preparation is made difficult by the start of the "holiday season" at Thanksgiving and the anticipation of Christmas symbols and rituals for the entire month preceding December 25. So, for example, the Vatican commentary on the calendar tells us that the reason for the omission of the Gloria during

Advent is to make its reintroduction at Christmas more special.[21] "Our Advent assemblies keep a lower tone of joy so that liturgical celebrations will be fresh on Christmas."[22] But how fresh can they be when for weeks before Santas and Christmas trees have mixed with angels and Nativity scenes, and the shopping malls have been playing *ad nauseam* the same hymns that will first be used in church at the vigil service? It is little wonder that many people are ready to be done with Christmas just when the church begins celebrating it.[23]

The difficulty of observing the liturgical seasons fully is exacerbated by the fragmentation and the individualism of contemporary life. We have, in general, little sense of connection with a communal consciousness, other than that provided by the media. Hence, it is not surprising that people schedule their weddings and baptisms according to when they can reserve the catering hall or get the family together, not according to liturgists' ideas of what is appropriate for a particular church season. With increasing frequency the theoretical "meaning" of the liturgical seasons—coherent and beautiful as it may be—simply does not connect with the lives of contemporary people, even if they are fervently practicing Christians; much less if they are more marginally connected to the church.

In the light of such tensions, the "seasonal" approach to celebrating the mystery of Christ may appear less compelling than in former times. The church has in fact to a large degree accommodated its observance of the seasons to the contemporary world (the most striking example: the minimizing of the Lenten discipline). Nevertheless, if shorn of the remnants of the mythological mentality, the celebration of the liturgical seasons can be a fruitful opportunity for the preacher. The theological insight that the resurrection is the constant reference point for all of our celebrations brings a consequent recognition of the wholeness of the mystery of salvation. This permits us to speak to the contemporary mentality by emphasizing the "always and everywhere" of God's saving presence. It valorizes the "quotidian" and profane world as the place of encounter with God.[24]

At the same time, the variety of the seasons allows us to relate the central resurrection mystery to the different "limit situations" that are encountered in every life: for example, the experience of incompleteness and longing (Advent); the gratuity of life and love (Christmas); revelation through personal encounter (Epiphany); sin, suffering, and death (Lent); the experience of unexplained courage, hope, and communion (Pentecost), etc. Taken in their theological context, the liturgical seasons provide a structure for a "correlational" method in preaching, relating these limit situations—the "questions" inherent in the human condition—to God's salvific "answer" in Christ.

Hence the different seasons are not and need not be all-encompassing or exclusive in their scope. We celebrate penance during Lent, longing in Advent, joy at Christmas, not because these are appropriate "seasonal" moods that correspond to a stage in the mythic or dramatic re-living of a story, but precisely because they are all *permanent* features of Christian existence in the Spirit; and we celebrate all in the larger context of the resurrection message represented by every eucharist. It is true that any particular individual's life situation and psychic state may not be those that the community is emphasizing at the moment; but if the latter are placed in their proper theological context, they will have something to say to every person's life-experience as a whole. The church's seasons also serve as a corrective to the superficiality and the commercial focus of so many of our secular "seasons," which tend to neglect not only the deeper dimensions of human existence, but also its negative moments of sorrow and suffering. Moreover, the concentration on particular sequential themes can serve as an antidote to the extreme individualism and rootlessness in the contemporary spirit. It opens us to the experiences of others and it provides a communal point of reference for reflection on life's great issues, seen in the perspective of God's revelation in Christ, known in the Spirit.

Advent and Lent: History and Meaning

The seasons of Advent and Lent fit together both in their historical origins (Advent having been patterned on Lent) and in their common nature as times of preparation. A brief consideration of the nature of the two seasons will serve as a prelude to an overview of the themes that run through their liturgical readings.

The season of Lent originated in a fast of one or two days in preparation for the celebration of the Christian pasch. Over the course of several centuries, the fast was extended to six days, and eventually to six weeks or forty days. From the end of the second century, penitential practice and fasting existed in the West. By the beginning of the fourth century, the idea of a forty-day fast in preparation for Easter was established in the Orient.[25] This number of fast days was determined by multiple symbolic associations from the Scriptures: Noah's salvation from the waters in the ark, a symbol of baptism (Gen 7:4ff.); Moses' sojourn before God on Mount Sinai (Ex 24:15ff.); the forty years of Israel in the desert (Ex 6:35); and, of course, Jesus' forty days of fasting and prayer in the wilderness (Mk 1:13; Mt 4:2; Lk 4:2). The development of the season was somewhat slower in the West. There the fast was extended to three weeks only in the sixth century; and only in the seventh century did Rome adopt the Oriental custom of a forty-day period of fasting.

The Lenten fast was severe. The spirit of the season was

originally determined by two groups: catechumens preparing for baptism at the Easter Vigil (at which the sacrament was celebrated from the beginning of the third century[26]) and public penitents preparing for discipline and reconciliation (which by the fifth century was held on the morning of Holy Thursday[27]). In association with these two groups, the season became for the whole church a time of repentance and of remembrance of baptism, as well as a preparation for Easter. During the Middle Ages both the catechumenate and the practice of public penance eventually disappeared as institutions. The Lenten fast remained, but with a changed focus. The folk piety centered on personal sharing in Christ's passion, already associated with the last week, was now extended to the whole of Lent,[28] which thus became increasingly a time of private asceticism within the framework of the church's discipline.

After the modern restoration of the Easter Vigil liturgy, the association of the Lenten season with baptism once more came to the fore: its purpose is to remind us that we have died with Christ in baptism, in order to live more fully.[29] The Second Vatican Council's *Constitution on the Sacred Liturgy* explicitly returns Lent to its original baptismal and penitential framework:

> The two elements which are especially characteristic of Lent—the recalling of baptism or the preparation for it, and penance—should be given greater emphasis in the liturgy and in liturgical catechesis. It is by means of them that the Church prepares the faithful for the celebration of Easter . . .[30]

The restitution of the catechumenate in the Rite of Christian Initiation for Adults and the restoration of public celebrations of penance[31] have strengthened the baptismal and penitential meanings of the season.

The origins of Advent are somewhat uncertain and confused. The Christmas cycle began independently of Easter, as a Christian response to the pagan festival of *Sol Invictus,* the celebration of the rebirth of the sun in the dark days of winter. As a result of the theological disputes of the fourth and fifth centuries, the feast of Christ's birth took on particular significance as an affirmation of the reality of the incarnation. Toward the end of the fourth century, a four- or six-week period of preparation was introduced, following the model of the Lenten preparation for Easter.[32] By the mid-fifth century the season was practiced in Antioch and Ravenna, but was still unknown in the Gallican liturgy. By mid-sixth century, the practice was adopted at Rome.[33] The usage never took hold in the Oriental church, which has only a brief preparation of a few days before Christmas.[34]

From the beginning of the fourth century, there were two distinct foci for Advent: on the one hand, it prepared for the feast of Christ's birth; on the other, for his eschatological coming. It is disputed which, if either, of these themes was more ancient. In any case, the two could easily be related, since the birth of Christ was celebrated precisely as the beginning of our salvation, and not for its own sake (hence not as a "birthday" in the modern sense).[35]

The liturgy of Advent evolved from the sixth to the eighth centuries, under the influence of already existing Lenten practices. Baptisms were often celebrated at Epiphany; Advent was used, like Lent, to prepare for them. Fasting was a feature of the season from early on (there was a fast of three days a week in the sixth century). Some areas practiced a comparatively mild discipline in preparation for the feast of the incarnation; others had a stricter observance,

emphasizing penance as a preparation for the last judgment.[36] In the Middle Ages Advent practices included conversion, fasting, and special preaching.[37] A major influence
in the development of the season was St. Bernard of Clair-
vaux's idea of the three "advents" of Christ: his birth; his
presence in us now; and his return in judgment.[38]

The liturgical reform following the Second Vatican
Council presumes a double focus for Advent.[39] In the Missal
of Paul VI, the season is divided into two parts: for the first
three Sundays and the weekdays until December 16th there
is an eschatological theme, while the fourth Sunday and the
weekdays from December 17th to the 24th center on preparation for Christmas.[40]

Although until modern times Advent was seen as a penitential as well as an anticipatory season, in many ways parallel to Lent,[41] present Roman documents do not refer to it as
a time of penance, but as one of "devout and joyful expectation."[42] Nevertheless, insofar as it has an eschatological focus and orients us to a future reality, Advent's message has
an intrinsically "ascetical" aspect: in speaking of promise and
awaiting, it implies detachment from the incompleteness of
the present and conversion to a more ultimate good.

The Cycles of Readings

The readings for Advent and Lent are carefully ar-
ranged in thematic sequence. They therefore provide the
opportunity for an "intratextual" approach to preaching:
one that sees the scriptural passages in relation to each
other, and expounds from them a coherent view of the
world and of human life. In order to speak to contemporary
Christians, however, such an approach must be combined
with a "correlational" method: one that critically examines
the Scriptures and the traditional Christian world-view from

the perspective of historical scholarship and relates it to the contemporary situation, including people's present experiences. The two elements—the scripturally-based Christian tradition and our life experience—shed light upon each other, interpret each other, and constitute God's present revelation to us. The preacher's role is to assist in this process, especially in interpreting and reflecting on the liturgical readings. Therefore, although the theme for any single homily may be determined more by the situation of a particular congregation or by current issues and events than by a preconceived sequence of themes, it is nevertheless useful for the preacher to have a sense of the overall direction of the seasonal readings.

In Advent, the structure of the thematic sequence of the gospel readings is the same for all three cycles. The first Sunday sets an eschatological tone, with readings concerning the sudden coming of God's judgment (years A and C: Jesus' warning of the unexpected coming of the Son of Man in Matthew and Luke; year B: the parable of the master who returns unannounced). These readings are taken to refer to Christ's return in glory at the end of time.[43] The second and third Sundays of all cycles present John the Baptist's call to conversion in the face of the coming judgment, and his testimony to Christ. On the fourth Sunday the theme changes to the birth of Christ, with readings from the infancy narratives presenting the prelude to the event (cycle A: Matthew's account of how the birth of Jesus came about; cycle B: the annunciation, from Luke; cycle C: the visitation, also from Luke).

The Old Testament readings for the season are taken from prophecies related to the Messiah or the messianic age. The book of Isaiah, which was traditionally used in Advent, provides all the readings for year A and three of the four in year B; the rest are taken from various prophets. All these readings have in common a theme of hope in God's future glorious and saving rule. On two Sundays there is a quotation of the first reading (prophecy) in the gospel (fulfillment): Isaiah's voice crying in the desert "prepare the way of the Lord," applied by Mark to John the Baptist (second Sunday, B); and the prophecy of the virgin who will be with child, applied by Matthew to the conception of Jesus (fourth Sunday, A). On the remaining Sundays, the relationship is indirect: the Old Testament readings, which envisage God's Kingdom, are referred by the church to Jesus as Messiah, either in his earthly mission or in his second coming.

The Advent second readings are taken from the New Testament letters, mostly from the Pauline corpus. They contain "exhortations and instructions on different themes of this season."[44] These readings emphasize the attitudes and conduct of Christians as they await the final coming of the Lord. Only on the fourth Sunday is there a reference to Jesus' birth or mission (year A, from Paul's letter to the Romans: Jesus, descended from David in the flesh, is the Son of God; year B, from Romans: the mystery hidden for ages is now manifest in the good news about Christ; year C, from the letter to the Hebrews: Jesus came into the world to do God's will).

The predominance of eschatological themes in the Advent readings—including those in which the Baptist identifies Jesus as the awaited one—allows the preacher to focus on the existential reality of awaiting Christ's final coming. Advent then centers on a real and present hope, rather than merely on the dramatic re-living of the messianic longings of the ancient Jews that have already been fulfilled (according to Christian interpretation) in Jesus. As Joseph Ratzinger puts it:

> The first thing that we must accept, over and over, is Advent as a permanent reality. If we do this, we will

begin to realize that the boundary between "before Christ" and "after Christ" does not run through history in an external way, and cannot be drawn on a map; rather, it goes through our own hearts. Insofar as we live out of egotism and selfishness, we today are still living "before Christ." But in this time of Advent we wish to ask our Lord that he will allow us to live ever less and less "before" Christ—and not to live "after" Christ, either, but genuinely to live *with* Christ and in Christ: with him, who is the same Christ yesterday, today, and forever (Heb 13:8).[45]

In this way, we avoid making of Advent a merely "seasonal" phenomenon, threatened by the competition of the secular world, and instead recognize its permanent relevance to our condition before God.

The cycles of Lenten readings are strongly thematic in structure. The gospels for the first Sunday are the synoptic accounts of Jesus' fasting and temptation—an introduction to the season and an example for Christians and prospective Christians entering into it.[46] On the second Sunday, we read the transfiguration story—a prefiguration of Jesus' death and resurrection, and a sign of hope for us, his disciples.

The gospels for the remaining Sundays of year A are especially oriented to Christian initiation, and may be used in any year, especially in connection with the instruction of catechumens who are to be baptized at Easter.[47] They are all taken from the gospel of John: the conversion of the Samaritan woman at the well, the cure of the blind man at the pool of Siloam, and the raising of Lazarus. The gospels of year B are also all from John, and center on the theme of Jesus' glorification through his death and rising:[48] the cleansing of the temple, Jesus' discourse with Nicodemus ("God so loved the world . . ."), and Jesus' prayer on entering into his "hour." The Sundays of year C stress the penitential side of Lent, with passages on conversion and forgiveness: Luke's account of Jesus' call for repentance, with the parable of the barren fig tree; the Lucan parable of the forgiving father and his two sons; and the story from John of the woman caught in adultery.[49]

The Old Testament readings for Lent present principal moments in the history of salvation, "from the beginning to the promise of the new covenant."[50] The first Sunday gives us stories from Genesis in years A and B (the creation and first sin of humanity; and the covenant with Noah after the flood), while in year C we read the Deuternomic confession of faith, recounting God's saving deeds from Abraham to the Exodus. In all three cycles the second Sunday centers on Abraham (his calling in year A; the sacrifice of Isaac in year B; the covenant in year C) and the third Sunday on Moses (giving water in the desert [year A]; receiving the ten commandments [year B]; encountering God in the burning bush [year C]). The fourth Sunday presents various later episodes in Israel's history: the annointing of David, from 1 Samuel (year A); the account from 2 Chronicles of Israel's infidelity, leading to the Exile and return (year B); and the celebration of the Passover in the promised land, from the book of Joshua (year C). The readings of the fifth Sunday are all from the prophets, and contain the promise of new life: Ezekiel's prophecy of the "resurrection" of Israel by God's spirit after the Exile (year A); Jeremiah's prophecy of a new covenant (year B); and Isaiah's prophecy of a new act of salvation by God (year C).

The second readings for Lent were chosen to harmonize as much as possible with the gospel and/or Old Testament readings. More than in any other time of the year, therefore, the three readings for each Sunday (and sometimes even the responsorial psalm) both form a progressive sequence from Sunday to Sunday and are thematically united among themselves. Thus, for example, on the first Sunday of year A, Paul's comparison of Christ and Adam from the letter to the

Romans unites the Genesis story of the fall with the gospel of Jesus' temptation. In year B, the story of Noah (first Sunday) is complemented by the use of the flood as a symbol of baptism in 1 Peter; the account of Abraham's sacrifice of Isaac (second Sunday) is followed by Paul's declaration of confidence in salvation because of the handing over God's own Son for us; and so on.

These multiple cross-references and associations can profitably be used by the preacher to expound a coherent theological vision of salvation. At the same time, they invite us to find in our own lives the openness to corresponding experiences of God's victorious saving grace. Like Advent, Lent is a time of expectation. It does not look only backward, to a history of salvation that has been completed by Christ's resurrection. For that event is by its nature eschatological, and in that sense is ongoing into what is for us the future. It anticipates our final incorporation into God's victorious rule; and it therefore confronts us with the always present reality of a call awaiting our response.

NOTES

[1] See, *inter alia, A History of Religious Ideas,* translated by Willard R. Trask, vol. 1 (Chicago: University of Chicago Press, 1978).

[2] Ibid., 42.

[3] It should be recalled, however, that Hinduism and Buddhism are very complex and embrace many different philosophical currents, not all of which "devalue" historical experience. Moreover, the illusory or unsubstantial character of the world is relative; in some forms of these religions, historical existence can be seen as a means to reaching or realizing the transcendental absolute. I believe it is therefore an oversimplification to contrast the "Christian" view of time to "the illusion of an etherial nirvana" as is

done, for example, by Achille Triacca. See s.v. "Tempo e liturgia" in *Nuovo Dizionario di Liturgia,* ed. Domenico Sartore, CSJ, and Achille M. Triacca, SDB (Roma: Edizioni Paoline, 1984).

[4] For a discussion of contemporary scientific speculation about time, see Raymond Flood and Michael Lockwood, eds.: *The Nature of Time* (Oxford: Basil Blackwell, 1986).

[5] For a discussion of the progressive "invention" of the modern concept of time, see Daniel J. Boorstin: *The Discoverers. A History of Man's Search To Know His World and Himself* (New York: Vintage Books, 1985), especially Book One, part two, "From sun time to clock time."

[6] Walter Kasper: *Jesus the Christ* (Ramsey, N.J.: Paulist Press, 1977), p. 77.

[7] The linear and eschatological view of time, although its "discovery" is sometimes attributed to the prophets of Israel, is not restricted to Judaism and Christianity. It is a major feature, for example, in the Zoroastrian world-view, which perhaps has its origins in a more ancient tradition common to the Indo-European peoples. See Eliade, *op, cit.* vol. 2, pp. 192ff. The "valorization" of history also takes place in other religious and philosophical systems, although on different grounds. See my *Answering for Faith. Christ and the Human Search for Salvation* (New York: Paulist Press, 1987), pp. 185ff.

[8] Contemporary science also formulates hypotheses about the possible "end" of the physical cosmos, for example in the eventual "heat death" of the universe through the working of the second law of thermodynamics. The relationship between such a hypothetical ending of the physical universe (or, alternatively, its physical "eternity" in an infinite series of "pulsations") on the one hand, and the theological notion of the "end," on the other, is a topic that has thus far received comparatively little consideration in the theological expositions of creation and eschatology. An exception is the work of Wolfhart Pannenberg. For his excellent treatment of the issue, see his *Systematic Theology,* vol. 2, trans. Geoffrey W. Bromily (Grand Rapids: William B. Eerdmans Publishing Company, 1994), pp. 146–161.

⁹ For a discussion of contemporary views of the uniqueness of Christ, see *Answering for Faith,* pp. 232ff.; also my article, "How Is Christ Absolute? Rahner's Christology and the Encounter of World Religions" in *Philosophy and Theology* II (Spring 1988): 220–40, and the literature there cited.

¹⁰ For an examination of the different dimensions of New Testament usage, see *s.v.* καιρός in G. Kittel and G. Friedrich (eds.): *Theological Dictionary of the New Testament.*

¹¹ The "proleptic" presence of the eschaton is a major theme in the theology of Wolfhart Pannenberg. See his exposition of the "retroactive force" of the eschaton in his *Jesus—God and Man,* trans. Lewis L. Wilkins and Duane A. Priebe (Philadelphia: Westminster Press, 1975), pp. 135ff., 141, and further explicitation in his *Systematic Theology,* vol. 2, p. 303, n. 92.

¹² *Presbyterorum Ordinis,* n. 5, in Austin Flannery, O.P. (ed.), *Vatican Council II. The Conciliar and Post Conciliar Documents* (Northport, N.Y.: Costello Publishing Co., 1975), p. 871.

¹³ *Sacrosanctum Concilium,* ch. V, no. 106, in Flannery, *op. cit.,* p. 30.

¹⁴ "Whenever the community gathers to celebrate the Eucharist, it announces the death and resurrection of the Lord, in the hope of his glorious return. The supreme manifestation of this is the Sunday assembly." S.C.R., *Eucharisticum Mysterium,* 25 May 1967, ch. II, in Flannery, *op. cit.,* p. 117.

¹⁵ *Sacrosanctum Concilium,* ch. V, no. 102, in Flannery, *op. cit.,* p. 29.

¹⁶ Augusto Bergamini, s.v. "anno liturgico" in *Nuovo Dizionario di Liturgia,* p. 66.

¹⁷ Ibid., p. 69.

¹⁸ "General Norms for the Liturgical Year and the Calendar," 1, in the *Roman Missal.*

¹⁹ *The Liturgical Year: Celebrating the Mystery of Christ and His Saints* (Washington, DC: United States Catholic Conference, 1985), 9. (Document from Bishops' Committee on the Liturgy, National Conference of Catholic Bishops).

²⁰ Ibid., 14.

21 Ibid., 40

22 Ibid.

23 The secular celebration of Christmas without an Advent is of course all the more problematic if one thinks of the liturgical seasons in "mythic" terms as a reliving of the events of sacred history. If Advent is intended as a dramatic re-enacting of the awaiting of the Messiah's birth, it is frustrating to have the climax of the drama repeatedly anticipated before the end is reached.

24 Bergamini, *art. cit.*, p. 66.

25 Balthasar Fischer, s.v. "Quadragesima" in Höfer, Josef and Rahner, Karl (eds.), *Lexikon für Theologie und Kirche* (Freiburg: Verlag Herder, 1963), vol. 8, col. 910–911.

26 Bergamini, *op. cit.*, p. 66.

27 Ibid.

28 Fischer, *op. cit.*, col. 910–911.

29 Ibid.

30 *Sacrosanctum Concilium,* #109, in Flannery, *op. cit.*, p. 30.

31 "The practice of penance should be not only internal and individual but also external and social." Ibid.

32 Bergamini, *op. cit.*, p. 66.

33 W. Croce and M-L. Lechner, s.v. "Advent" in Höfer and Rahner, *op. cit.*, vol. 1, 160–161.

34 A. Bergamini, s.v. "Avvento" in Sartore and Triacca, *op. cit.*, p. 137.

35 Croce and Lechner, *op. cit.*, col. 160–161.

36 *The Liturgical Year,* p. 39.

37 Croce and Lechner, *op. cit.*, col. 160–161.

38 *The Liturgical Year,* p. 39.

39 "Advent has a twofold character: as a season to prepare for Christmas when Christ's first coming to us is remembered; as a season when that remembrance directs the mind and heart to await Christ's second coming at the end of time." "General Norms for the Liturgical Year and the Calendar," #38.

40 Ibid.

41 Although the Advent fast was abolished in modern times by the Code of Canon Law, some liturgical parallels to Lent remained even after the Second Vatican Council: for example, the use of

purple vestments; the omission of the "Glory to God"; even the prohibition of solo instrumental music (S.C.R., "Instruction on Music in the Liturgy," 5 March, #66, in Flannery, *op. cit.,* p. 96).

[42] "General Norms for the Liturgical Year and the Calendar," #38.

[43] See the Introduction to the Lectionary for Mass, ch. II.

[44] Ibid.

[45] Joseph Ratzinger: *Vom Sinn des Christseins. Drei Predigten* (München: Kösel Verlag, 1965), p. 34 (my translation).

[46] For candidates in the RCIA, the first Sunday of Lent celebrates the rite of election and inscription of names.

[47] The third through fifth Sundays of Lent mark the "scrutinies" of the catechumens in the RCIA, and the readings are particularly adapted to their progression toward initiation.

[48] This is how the theme is characterized in the introduction to the lectionary. In connection with the first readings for this cycle, one might also emphasize the theme of Jesus' death and rising as the new covenant.

[49] It is notable that in a number of important manuscripts, this story also occurs in the gospel of Luke, rather than in John. If this placement is correct, then the entire series of gospels for year C is from Luke. With regard to this gospel passage, Raymond Brown remarks that "stylistically, the story is more Lucan than Johannine." Brown holds that the passage was in any case not originally a part of John's gospel. For a discussion of its provenance, see his *The Gospel According to John, I–XII* (Garden City: Doubleday and Co., 1966), p. 336.

[50] Introduction to the Lectionary, ch. II.

First Sunday of Advent—Year A

Is 2:1–5
Ps 122:1–2, 3–4, 4–5, 6–7, 8–9
Rom 13:11–14
Mt 24:37–44

On the bulletin board of a school I recently saw a sign that read: "What a great world it would be if schools had all the money they needed, and the Air Force had to hold bake sales to buy a bomber."

Most of us would probably agree that it would be a much better world; but it is fairly clear that not many people in our country would actually vote for a candidate who promised to plan the federal budget on that basis.

In front of the United Nations Building in New York is a statue that represents the famous verse from the prophet Isaiah in today's first reading. It portrays a heroic figure beating with a great hammer on a bent sword, whose end has already begun to take the shape of a plowshare. Again, most of us would probably agree that this symbolizes a wonderful idea: turning the instruments of destruction into instruments of productivity. But how many would favor abandoning our country's arsenal of weapons in favor of ecological and agricultural research to feed the starving people of the world? All of us presumably share in seeing the beauty of the vision of justice and peace; but not all believe that the vision can be made real in this world. The point is illustrated in a recent *New Yorker* cartoon. A preacher proclaims to his congregation: "And the Lord said: 'They shall gradually, so as not to cause unemployment, beat their swords into plowshares.'"

For many, the biblical ideal of peace prophesied by Isaiah is simply not "realistic." That it does not fit with the realities of the present American economy is obvious; but this is only a sign of a more fundamental problem. Many would hold that on a deeper level, such a vision is incompatible with the basic realities of the human condition itself, to which conflict and hostility are endemic—perhaps even an evolutionary necessity, implanted in our genes.

There are some, in fact, who base their pessimism about the world precisely on their Christian faith. They emphasize that we live in a world infected by "original sin" and its effects, as well as by personal evil; in such a world, we may admire ideals of goodness, but in living we must be "realistic"; we must deal with the imperfect world as it is, and must take measures—unfortunate as they may be—to defend ourselves and fight against its evil. The prophet's vision will be realized in heaven, not on earth.

Another sort of Christianity has quite a different attitude. It does not disagree about the fact of sin or the need to be realistic. But it defines realism in a different way; it holds that true realism means believing not only in what is, but also in what can be. It believes in sin, but also in grace, and does not think that the latter is less "real" than the former. It sees the darkness; but it believes that a light has broken through.

In practical terms there is a great difference. Do we simply deal with the world as it is, or do we expect to change it—however slowly, however little? Do we live by what now is, or by what is possible—by a vision of the future?

There can be no doubt that Christianity in its origins was a visionary religion. Today's readings give us some sense of its eschatological expectation. Christians were to live in anticipation, orienting their lives not to the present, but to the world's imminent change. St. Paul tells the Romans to "make no provision for the desires of the flesh," human sin and weakness. They are to be, by worldly standards, utterly "unrealistic." Jesus tells his disciples to live with a continual preparedness for the "coming" of the Son of Man, the agent of God's judgment, and the ending of the world of ordinary affairs.

Most Christians probably think that it is possible to live that way—in a monastery or a convent. In fact, many people presume that nuns and priests live a "godly" life precisely by being sheltered from the "real" world, so that they can remain in a never-never-land of child-like innocence all their lives. Ordinary people, on the other hand, must compromise; they must be realistic; they must make provisions for the desires of the flesh.

There is, however, another possibility: to live in the everyday world, facing its evil conditions, not expecting an immediate solution by God's sudden coming, but stubbornly clinging to the vision and the possibility of building God's Kingdom among us. The great thing about the statue in front of the United Nations is that it portrays the prophecy not completed, but in process; the sword is still there, but the plowshare is slowly being hammered out of it.

The season of Advent is a reminder for us that the Christian life is one of hope: not merely hope for after death, nor hope for a miraculous transformation by divine intervention from beyond the world, but hope based on the power of love to create a new reality from within. It is notable that the "realism" which thinks that the world cannot be changed for the better occurs with great frequency among those whose interests lie in preserving the status quo. The poor and oppressed can't afford that kind of "realism"; if their spirits are not to be deadened and their lives totally dehumanized, they need to hope. Conversely, those who hope for humanity and dedicate themselves to making that hope real will inevitably end up—like Jesus—in some way suffering with the poor and oppressed: the "real" world will reject them as dreamers, idealists, people to be taken advantage of. The person who hopes walks into this with eyes open and a joyous heart. The coming that we await is already real within us, and through us—even in the long struggle, even in our apparent failures—is making a new reality present in the world.

First Sunday of Advent—Year B

Is 63:17, 19; 64:2–7
Ps 80:2–3, 15–16, 18–19
1 Cor 1:3–9
Mk 13:33–37

At the beginning of one Advent in the seminary, as we were putting up wreaths and other decorations in preparation for Christmas, a fellow faculty member suddenly turned to me and exclaimed, "How I hate this season!"

Does it seem strange that a priest should hate Christmas, or at least the preparation for it? I think I know what he meant, and have heard similar feelings expressed many times. I took the remark to be an expression of the tension between what Christmas *ought* to mean and be for a person of faith, and what it has actually become in our society.

Something of the same sentiment of disillusionment—albeit perhaps for different reasons—is expressed in Ogden Nash's poem, "I remember Yule":

I can even remember when Christmas was an occasion
    for fireside rejoicing and general good will,
And now it is just the day that it's only X shopping
    days until . . .

There is perhaps no clearer expression of the difference between being a Christian and living in a post-Christian society than the way one reacts to and prepares for Christmas.

The liturgy of Advent encourages us to feel a longing that has nothing to do with Christmas lists or material wants.

In a spirit contrary to the invitation of the commercial world around us, it invites us to interiority, introspection, purification, simplicity; it asks us to put first things first, to know what we are about.

The message of the "holiday" advertisements that now begin before Thanksgiving is: "feel the magic." We are urged to engage in a materialistic fantasy, to imagine ourselves the possessors of those sparkling consumer items, to get swept up in the illusion that having more things will make us happy, or that giving them will bring happiness to others.

The gospel's message to us is: "be awake!" To be wakeful is to be conscious, to know what is going on, not to be dreaming or living in illusion. Being awake spiritually means waiting, being in expectation of God, holding ourselves ready for God's coming. How? The parable makes it clear: we are to wait like servants. Waiting is not putting aside the tasks of life, but taking them up, being responsible.

The concrete meaning for us is that we must not allow ourselves to be put to sleep spiritually, hypnotized by the constant messages of frenetic grasping or drugged by heady but empty promises of pleasure. We must wait for God—by soberly, quietly taking responsibility for each other and our suffering world.

And this imperative to take responsibility is not merely an invitation to have a general attitude or a pious sentiment, but is a challenge to act in quite specific ways.

In a talk to ministers in Memphis, President Clinton addressed the issue of "the blight of crime, drugs, joblessness, and family disintegration." He might have added such things as the decline in educational standards and the widespread despair and aimlessness among young people in our society. The President rejoiced that many people now recognize that the essential problem is a moral one: a general lack of values and purpose. Moreover, people want change: a moral revolution. But, as columnist Peter Steinfels pointed out in his comments on the President's address, a major question remains unanswered: who will be willing to make the sacrifices needed for such a revolution to take place?[1]

We see over and over again how difficult it is to change public policy when the interests of some group are threatened. Change is even more difficult when the "moral revolution" demands real sacrifices in terms of our accustomed "lifestyle." Steinfels asks: is the entertainment industry ready "to take seriously the possibility that an environment saturated with images of sex and violence might be linked to the self-destructive behavior of 15-year olds?" More to the point: are *we* ready to take it seriously? Perhaps we agree with the idea; but do we turn off the programs? Do we avoid renting the videos? Do we refuse to allow the TV to become an easy way to take the children off our busy hands? Do we write to the manufacturers of violent toys?

But even such individual efforts, important as they are, do not suffice. It is not enough simply to denounce and reject the culture of violence and sex that has grown around us. More fundamentally, what are we doing about the pervasive culture of consumption, of greed, of materialism, of immediate gratification, that underlies their appeal?

The problem finally cannot be solved by prohibitions— on either the legal or personal levels. One cannot legislate "values," for a country or for one's own family. In the last analysis they can only be communicated as a matter of conviction: those who hold them must show that living virtuously, unselfishly, is not only possible, but is desirable. Are we ready to show a way of living that can compete with the values of sex, violence, pleasure, manipulation, and greed?

This is the real challenge of Advent's call to be awake and alert. Not only to be aware in mind, but to be active in knowing and doing good, and doing it with the joy that comes from conviction. Only the example of such joy can finally convince anyone else that what we preach is worth listening to and seeking.

NOTE

[1] *New York Times,* Nov. 27, 1993.

First Sunday of Advent—Year C

Jer 33:14–16
Ps 25:4–5, 8–9, 10, 14
1 Thes 3:12–4:2
Lk 21:25–28, 34–36

At the start of today's liturgy we performed a ceremony repeated in churches and homes throughout the world: the lighting of a candle, the symbol of Advent. The single small flame, burning alone in the midst of the others yet unlit, reminds us that this is a feast of beginnings, of waiting and anticipation.

It may at first seem strange that the gospel of this liturgy of beginnings turns our attention to the end: to the coming of the heavenly judge, the Son of Man (Dan 7:13f.), identified by the church with Christ in his "second" and glorious appearance. But it is the very nature of a beginning to initiate a process or a journey toward an anticipated goal, the journey's end and purpose. For this reason our celebration of beginnings reminds us first of the end that is still ahead of us, toward which we are still on our way. In so doing it leads us to reflect on the profound dimensions of our Advent season as a whole.

In its most obvious meaning, Advent is of course a preparation for Christmas, the feast of Jesus' birth. We are invited to feel the meaning of that feast more profoundly by reflecting on the history of humanity, and especially of the Jewish people, awaiting a salvific act of God. In this way, Advent can be thought of as a kind of dramatic device, in which we imagine ourselves sharing the anticipation of a future savior, so that on Christmas the past "arrival" of Christ may be felt by us as present, and so occur anew in our hearts by opening them to its meaning and influence.

But in a more profound sense, Advent is not merely an emotive recalling of the past history of salvation. It is possible and legitimate for us to enter into an imaginative longing for Christ precisely because there is in us a *real* longing, an expectation of salvation still to come. Otherwise, Advent would be mere play-acting. Jesus' birth, our liturgy reminds us, is itself not simply the end of anticipation and longing; in a sense, it is rather the deepening of it. The "coming" of the Christ event, in its full dimension, is not complete with Jesus' birth, nor even with his historic life, death, and resurrection; its glorious fulfillment, in which we are included, still remains future. It is for this reason that we declare at every eucharist that "we wait in joyful hope for the coming of our Savior Jesus Christ." Advent is the season of our most explicit awareness of that waiting and that hope.

Our times are perhaps particularly in need of this Advent message. We are peculiarly aware of the ambiguity of the future. Actual and potential crises abound: wars and conflicts, large and small, given a new menace by the instability following the breakup of Communism; the increasing proliferation of nuclear technology among rival powers; the contamination of environment, threatening changes in climate that may affect the earth's productivity; the menace of economic collapse due to poor management at home and throughout the world; tensions and terrorism that are the legacy of injustice and exploitation; increasing crime stemming in part from the alienation and despair of large sectors of society; new diseases arising and old ones once thought conquered reaching epidemic proportions. Many young people wonder whether humanity has a future, whether there is anything to hope for.

In this situation there occurs another danger, not less significant: that of refusing to face the future, of attempting to escape from the uncertainty of life—social and individual—by living only for the material satisfactions of the present moment. In today's gospel Jesus warns against this danger: "be on guard lest your spirits become bloated with indulgence and drunkenness and worldly cares . . ."

The temptation is particularly acute in a materialistic society, where the lives of many are dehumanized not by poverty, but by abundance. While visiting a family recently, I saw several young children sitting in front of a television, watching a "childrens'" channel. During each of the frequent commercials—all of them advertising toys—they would cry out, "I want that! I want that!" Around them, the family room was littered on all sides with forgotten toys and half-dismembered games. The situation struck me as a parable for much of our society. Dr. Jonas Salk once said that we are living in a sea of overproduction, with the result that we are too busy coping with things to have any room in our lives for depth, for reflection or expression. But the superficiality of escapism is ultimately destructive: for when one recognizes the emptiness and sameness of one's toys, as one surely must sooner or later, one ends with having nothing worthy of human life, and little capacity for any true joy. Is it surprising that we find so much confusion, disillusionment and despair about us?

In this situation, in the face of incertitude and anxiety, it is the task of Christians to light the flame of hope. If we look at the history of the tragedies and sufferings of human life, it is almost miraculous that such a flame still burns—flickering and fragile, seemingly in danger of being extinguished by the least breath; but nevertheless secure.

We have this secure hope because of God. Whatever may be the human future of the world, there is an absolute future for each individual and for all creation: all things go to an end. Perhaps it is precisely this—the subconscious anticipation and fear of the end—that causes terror and anxiety, and tempts us to seek escape. But that absolute future has revealed itself to us. This is the meaning of death and resurrection of Jesus, and the reason for our hope. We have experienced our future, and it is love. This is the reason why our hope is in fact more lasting and more real than any of the forces of history—and why it can give us the courage to face the future with open eyes and joyous hearts.

The lighting and preserving of the flame of hope is the task of all Christians. When we gather at the eucharist, we signify our hope by giving thanks: we see the past that we commemorate as leading forward and giving life. When we share fellowship, peace, and communion, what we await is present among us: the love that is origin and end of all things is present as our nourishment. It lights in us the Advent flame: light and warmth for our hearts, a sign of hope for the world.

In practice, that hope is also the act of love. We can only feel the reality of what hope promises if we are already living it; and what our hope promises is love, as ground and goal of all things. We know that what we hope is true, because it is already transforming our lives; we taste the eternity of love in the love we now share. Those who live in love have reason to hope; they give reasons to hope; they *are* reason to hope.

Second Sunday of Advent—Year A

Is 11:1–10
Ps 72:1–2, 7–8, 12–13, 17
Rom 15:4–9
Mt 3:1–12

The Benedictine Dom Bede Griffiths tells a story from his years in India about one of the monks who was serving as parish priest in the neighborhood of the monastery:

> There was a school attached to the parish, and one day he went up to a group of children and asked them, "Where is God?" Some were Catholics and some were Hindus. All the Catholic children pointed up: God is in Heaven. All the Hindu children pointed to their breasts: God is in the heart.[1]

The anecdote illustrates a significant feature of the biblical tradition in general, and is relevant to our Advent season in particular: if we await the "coming" of God, it is presumably because God is—in some sense—not "here." Certainly we acknowledge the universal presence of God, the divine "indwelling"; but is it not true that we usually think of God as being distant or even absent from the world? Transcendence is thought of in terms of God's being "not here" or "not yet."

This has important implications for our religious attitudes. Thus, for example, scholars point out that while the Hindu term for "peace," *shanti,* means "rest, repose" (i.e., an acceptance of the present), the Hebrew word *shalom,* the

39

"peace" promised by the prophets and spoken of in our psalm, connotes the putting right of wrongs: a *future* reality that must *happen.*

The prophetic tradition sees that peace as an eschatological event, a result of the intervention or the "coming" of God at the end of time and the establishment of God's rule through a messianic figure, an ideal King. In today's gospel, John the Baptizer appears as the culmination of that tradition, announcing God's impending arrival to purify the world with the eschatological fire which will bathe ("baptize") the world, a fire which itself is God's "breath" or "spirit." (The authenticity of this gospel saying is supported by the fact that a similar saying about the eschaton occurs in the Qumran writings: "God will cleanse them by a holy spirit from all evil deeds.")

While the Baptizer stresses the need for conversion and warns of the fate of those who do not reform, the first reading, from Isaiah, gives a magnificent vision of the peace, justice, and right that will come about through the coming Messiah. The poor will have justice; there will be universal knowledge and prosperity and an end to violence and fear; even nature will partake in the reconciliation of all things in this vision of the "peaceable Kingdom":

> the wolf shall be a guest of the lamb, and the
> leopard shall lie down with the kid;
> the calf and the young lion shall browse together,
> with a little child to guide them.

But while the vision is still heart-moving, one wonders whether we can or do still believe in it. Most modern people seem to have abandoned the hope for an imminent divine coming; and we are suspicious of utopian visions and prophetic warnings alike. Woody Allen expresses this skepticism in his version of Isaiah's famous prophecy: the lion will lie down with the lamb, but the lamb will get very little sleep. We have perhaps a healthy "realism" about ideologies that promise a paradise on earth, as well as about humanity and its possibilities.

But what happens, then, to our sense of expectation, our Advent hope for God's coming? Is it reduced to a fiction, a cyclical commemoration of a *past* expectation that was fulfilled at Christ's birth—a preparation for the feast of Christmas, and nothing more? Is there anything for *us* to hope for and await? Or is the object of our expectation put off to "another" world, an afterlife?

The Christian proclamation is that the awaited arrival of God's messianic savior and God's transforming, purifying Spirit *has* occurred—*and* is still occurring. God's victorious presence is real as the dynamism in our lives, the reason for our hope and our action. We could not be seeking God "in the Kingdom" unless God were already present in our hearts; it is precisely because of the divine presence of God "within" that we can seek and long for God. For the Christian, the peace of God is both a present reality and a promise; and because a promise, also a task and a challenge. The cleansing fire is already here; are we willing to allow ourselves to be burned, sifted, transformed, as a sign to the world of the secret presence that is also present within it, waiting to be discovered?

NOTE

[1] Bede Griffiths. *The Cosmic Revelation.* Springfield, Ill: Templegate, 1983; p. 24.

Second Sunday of Advent—Year B

Is 40:1–5, 9–11
Ps 85:9—10, 11–12, 13–14
2 Pt 3:8–14
Mk 1:1–8

Riding in the New York City subway recently, I looked around to observe the faces of my fellow passengers. It is something one does carefully on the subway; normally people there avoid looking at each other. Meeting another's eyes can be dangerous; a misinterpreted look could lead to confrontation, perhaps to violence—any New Yorker has at least read about it in the newspapers, has probably seen it happen. When people enter into those cars, they withdraw into themselves. Even people who have been conversing together on the platform seem to feel compelled to become silent. Entering the subway is like going on stage; people don't want to expose their private affairs in public. The faces I observed had become unmoving, masklike, showing no reactions. The eyes stare straight ahead, glazed, averted from contacts. Although everyone is on the same train, each is going on his or her own journey, isolated from the rest.

As I looked, I was reminded of something, but couldn't place what it was. Where had I seen such hard, silent faces, such empty gazes, before? Suddenly it came to me, with shock: in church!

I sometimes wonder whether the people in church have any notion of what the celebrant sees when he looks out on the congregation on Sunday morning. At most liturgies, I see many faces like those on the subway: faces that convey isolation, grimness, boredom. Of course, there are others as well: the silence of some people bespeaks devotion, prayer, meditation; there are expressions of peace and kindness, eyes that are clear and attentive. And there are some liturgies that are full of active participation and infectious joy. But too many church pews that I have seen look disconcertingly like the benches on the subway: the people sitting there are present physically, but their minds are elsewhere; they are essentially waiting to reach their stop and get out and get on with life.

How is it that the celebration of the eucharist has become for some people a burdensome duty, an interruption of life, rather than a vital part of life itself? How is it that the message of comfort and challenge spoken there seems so frequently to fail to engage them in their hearts? We could probably come up with many answers to this question, on different levels: the Catholic heritage of legalism and obligation fosters a mechanical attendance at mass; the structure of the liturgy and even the physical structure of our churches lend themselves easily to a "theatrical" presentation, where the clergy and ministers are active, and the congregation passive onlookers; historically, we lack a habit of participation; the liturgy is frequently poorly prepared, and is led without spirit or imagination; there is a problem of routine, with the repetition of the same prayers, gestures, and ceremonies week after week, year after year; people come to liturgy directly from the hectic concerns of life, and carry with them the depersonalized, functional attitude that characterizes most activities in our society; they are tired and unprepared for personal engagement on a deep level.

In this situation, perhaps we have a special need to proclaim and take to heart anew the Advent message proclaimed in today's scriptures: "prepare the way of the Lord!"

The "way" of the Lord is first of all God's way to us. The

prophet Isaiah (first reading) compares God's salvific coming to the triumphant arrival of an Oriental monarch, preceded by servants who remove every obstacle to the royal progress. The preparation of God's coming is on a cosmic scale: the very mountains and valleys will be leveled to become a smooth road. In the beginning to Mark's gospel, the idea is personalized: Mark sees John the Baptizer's call to repentance and conversion as the fulfillment of Isaiah's prophecy. The "way" to be prepared for God is in human hearts; the obstacles to be removed are those of human sinfulness.

How do we "prepare" this way in our time and place?

Even to be able to address the structural and personal manifestations of human sinfulness and its consequences, we must first be moved by the call; we must be convinced of the need to "prepare"; we must have an attitude of active attention and a willingness to be involved. This means the basic realization that our relation to God is not like a subway ride, in which a mysterious anonymous "soul" is passively carried along by "grace" or by the habits of religious life, to reach God only at the end. Rather, what happens in true religion—and what should happen in our liturgical celebrations—is intensely personal and inter-personal, and involves the wholeness of our historical being, in spirit and body, in relation to others and the world.

God wishes to come to us, to reach into the everyday reality of our lives; and we ourselves, in our most personal being, are to be the "way" of God's coming to ourselves and to each other. Thus God's "way" to us is also our way to God. In order to prepare that way—that is, consciously to *become* the locus and means of God's coming to the world—we must first overcome the passivity and lethargy that so frequently characterize the routine of our lives: not only our liturgies and our private prayer, but all the many aspects of daily existence that are so frequently lived in forgetfulness of

God. We must allow the message of God's real "coming," God's incessant loving initiative toward us, to penetrate to our hearts. To receive this Advent message is only the beginning: the work of flattening the mountains of alienation, leveling the valleys of human hopelessness, making life into a road with a clear direction, remains a lifelong task. But its beginning—or its re-beginning—for each of us can take place now.

Second Sunday of Advent—Year C

Bar 5:1–9
Ps 126:1–2, 2–3, 4–5, 6
Phil 1:4–6, 8–11
Lk 3:1–6

In an unfrequented corner of the Palatine Museum in Rome there is a collection of ancient graffiti. Most visitors give them no more than a glance before passing on to the more attractive statues and artifacts. Roughly etched on slabs of marble, these inscriptions once defaced the walls of the imperial palaces that stood on the spot. Among them is one with a very crudely drawn image and a few words of Greek that is called the "graffito of Alexamenos." In style and appearance it has nothing to distinguish it from the many other pieces around it; but for the Christian it has a particular significance. The crude incision shows a crucified man with the head of an ass. Next to him is a smaller figure with an arm extended in his direction. Nearby are the words, "Alexamenos worships his God." It is the first known representation of the crucifixion of Christ and of his adoration as divine. In a city so full of the triumphant monuments of Christianity, there is something strangely moving in finding this first visual testimony to the Christian faith amidst the fragments of daily life of pagan Rome; and even more so in finding it in this rude sketch, probably drawn by a palace page with cruel schoolboy humor to mock the faith of a fellow slave.

The graffito reminds us of how Christianity must have appeared to the sophisticated ancient pagan world: a strange minority religion from a small backwater of the civilized world, centered on a man punished as a criminal with the most humiliating form of execution, and practiced mostly by slaves and people of the lower classes.

In this context we may be struck by the boldness of Luke's purposeful setting of the beginnings of his gospel precisely in the perspective of world history, represented for him by the Roman Empire. Luke wishes to emphasize the universal significance of Jesus, and in doing so he exposes the great scandal of faith in Christ: that this particular man, in all the limitations of his history in space and time, is affirmed as God's final word of salvation for all humanity and for all ages.

The scandal of Jesus' historical particularity is in some sense perhaps even greater for us than for his contemporaries. Not only do we live over a thousand years after the demise of the whole political and social structure of the Roman Empire; but we are aware that that Empire is only one of many civilizations and cultures that have appeared, flourished, and disintegrated over the hundreds of thousands of years of human history. We come to the gospel with a historical consciousness that embraces the earth; an evolutionary consciousness that sees civilization as a comparatively recent phenomenon, occupying a chronologically small part of humanity's development; a cosmic consciousness that places the earth itself in the context of an unimaginably vast universe. For us, Luke's listing of Roman officials, far from putting the Christ story within the largest framework of universal history, serves to emphasize again its smallness within the total history of humankind, not to speak of the universe.

The more conscious we are of the extent and expanse of history, the more striking is the audaciousness of the Christian claim. Why should God's final word have come in *this* particular place and time, rather than in another? Why not in a place and time more developed, more universally accessible, more available to knowledge and communication? Indeed, why not universally, in every time and place equally?

The "scandal" of particularity is also—seen from the point of view of faith—the wonder of the incarnation: that God becomes truly human, and that therefore humanity—the very same humanity that we all share—is capable of being one with God's own life and "expressing" it, making it present in history. God's love and grace are universal: God's Spirit encounters us always and everywhere. But humanity is not pure universal spirit: for us, the transcendent and absolute is always mediated by the particular, the material, the historically limited and relative. If the message of the incarnation is true—if God does not remain the always-distinct horizon of our existence, but really meets us personally *in* our world—then that meeting must take place in accord with the human way of being in the world, which is always "located" in space and time, always particular. If God truly becomes human—that is, if God's always-and-everywhere love for humanity actually finds in history a triumphant moment of full acceptance and accomplishment in at least one human life—then that event must make present God's own life within the limitations of a particular human time and place and all the accidental circumstances—including material, social, cultural, and psychological contexts—that these imply.

This is a difficult message to accept, for it means accepting not only the real humanity of Christ, but also our own humanity. And many of us do not wish to be human. Perhaps we would like our religion to be more "mysterious," more other-worldly, less attached to the messy, complex realities of everyday life. Perhaps we would prefer a more majestic God, who becomes manifest in supernatural wonders and triumphal manifestations. But the Christian message—the message of Advent—directs our hearts toward humble humanity.

This does not mean that there is no glory, no mystery; but it means that we must seek them not in an external divine intrusion into the world, a triumphal interruption of human history, but rather in the transformation of that history from within by God's presence in human hearts.

In this sense, the entry of God into the world is not like a cosmic version of the grand processional progress of an Oriental king, as described in today's gospel in the passage from Isaiah that is applied to John the Baptizer. The valleys are not filled in, the mountains are not leveled; the crooked ways remain crooked, and the paths are still rough. The "landscape" of human existence remains, in one sense, unchanged by the incarnation. It is precisely here, in the ups and downs, in the winding and difficult roads of life, that we find the presence of God. Always—and not only in the case of faith in Jesus—our encounter with God is tied to particular times, places, events, persons; it is more present in some circumstances than in others; it depends upon human insight, freedom, and accomplishment, on the individual and the communal levels, as well as on the ever-present grace of God.

But this means also that there *is* a leveling and overturning to be accomplished in order to "make ready the way of the Lord": not a change from our human condition, but first of all a change in our hearts and minds, a conversion toward our humanity itself: the recognition of that humanity as capable of being the very abode of God, and the willing it to be such. And this in turn implies commitment to another level of preparation and removal of obstacles, in community and history: the overturning of all those conditions of suffering, injustice, ignorance, and hatred that dehumanize people and alienate them—oppressed and oppressors alike—from their own humanity. Only by committing ourselves to this process may we hope for the fulfillment of the prophet's vision that "all flesh shall see the salvation by our God."

Third Sunday of Advent—Year A

Is 35:1–6, 10
Ps 146:6–7, 8–9, 9–10
Jas 5:7–10
Mt 11:2–11

"The glory of Lebanon will be given to them . . ."

The words from our first reading were originally part of a prophecy of a victorious return of the enslaved people of Israel from the exile in Babylon. Later they were applied to the hopes of God's people for the establishment of the triumphant rule of God by the Messiah. Still later the entire prophecy was applied in a metaphorical sense to Christ; and it is in this sense that it figures in our liturgy.

But there is an unintended irony in our use of the phrase about the glory of Lebanon. It is used by the prophet as a symbol of the splendor of God's salvation. But the beauty of that country, fabled in the ancient world, today lies largely devastated by war, terrorism, and civil discord. Its people are divided by religious, national and racial hatred; its economy is in ruins; its political structure is anarchic. Far from making us think of an earthly paradise, Lebanon today brings to mind a series of nearly insoluble problems; it is a symbol of the sorrows of a divided and turbulent world.

The contrast between the scriptural prophecy and the current situation points to the continued relevance of the question asked of Jesus by John the Baptizer: "Are you he who is to come, or do we look for another?"

The response of Jesus in the gospel is to point to his actions. The events of God's Kingdom are happening: "the

50

blind see, cripples walk, lepers are healed, the deaf hear, the dead are raised to life, and the poor have good news preached to them." The messianic prophecies are fulfilled: therefore the Messiah has come.

But where are those saving actions for us—for the suffering people in Lebanon or Somalia or Northern Ireland or El Salvador; for the babies born with AIDS or those dying from cancer? As a student in one of my college classes asked me this week: "If Jesus is the savior, just where is the salvation?"

One common religious attitude would probably think that such questions entirely miss the point about salvation. Many Christians take it for granted that salvation refers to a reality that occurs on the other side of death. In this world, we are still awaiting and working out our eternal destiny. As the letter of James (second reading) says, we must suffer hardships patiently as we await the coming of the Lord.

There is of course a truth to this. We are in fact still waiting; Advent is not a fiction, but points to the real "not yet" of God's salvific action for us. We still pray, as in our response to today's psalm, "Lord, come and save us." If Jesus brought the Kingdom of God, it was in an unexpected way. The reality of salvation in this life is symbolized by the cross; the glorious fulfillment is yet to come.

Yet the cross of Jesus can have no salvific sense except in the light of the resurrection; it is this that allows us to proclaim that he is after all the one we are awaiting; it is this that permits us to claim that the power of the Kingdom has triumphed in history, despite the apparent failure of the messianic promise on the cross. It is true that salvation remains "future" for us. But our proclamation of the resurrection— which is the substance of every eucharistic celebration— means that the power of the future, of God's Kingdom in its glory, has already appeared in history. The resurrection means that the "reign" of God—that is, the triumph of

God's love for humanity—signified in Jesus' actions of healing, giving sight, bringing life—has entered the world in a definitive way, despite the power of sin expressed in the crucifixion. The resurrection is a reality only if this is true: if God's love has in fact triumphed and is at work in the world, in us, through God's spirit.

We would have no basis for hope of a salvation "beyond" this life unless the substance of that beyond—the reality of love—were already transforming us into loving people, people in whom our future of absolute love has already become active. And this transformation must also have an effect on the world. So the question—"If Jesus is the savior, where is the salvation?"—is a legitimate one. And we, like Jesus, should be able in reply to point to the works of salvation taking place. The signs of the messianic age: healing the sick, giving sight, bringing good news to the poor, should still be occurring—not miraculously, but through the life of Christ in us, inspiring us to use our intelligence and energy in finding solutions to the sufferings and lacks of human life. The final validation of Christ as savior must await the consummation in the Kingdom of God; but the signs of the reality of that Kingdom should be found in our commitment not only to the Lebanons and Somalias of the world, but to all of suffering humanity around us.

To the Baptizer's question we can then reply: no, we are not waiting for another; there is no other way to salvation than the love manifested in the message and the self-giving of Jesus. Nor are we simply waiting passively for that love to come in a future definitive way: we have been touched by it; we are being transformed; we commit ourselves to bringing it to each other.

Third Sunday of Advent—Year B

Is 61:1–2, 10–11
Lk 1:46–48, 49, 50, 53–54
1 Thes 5:16–24
Jn 1:6–8, 19–28

One major effect of the commercialization of Christmas is that every year the gap between Christmas and Thanksgiving seems to grow smaller. It is common now to hear Christmas carols in early December; by this time many people have not only bought but have also decorated their trees; Christmas parties abound in offices and places of business. Virtually the only place where one does not see Christmas cribs and hear Christmas carols is in church (a fact that must cause some confusion in the minds of young children). While secular society is frantically anticipating the feast and adapting it for its own purposes, the church obstinately says, "not yet."

In spite of the difficulty of being out of step with the surrounding society, the church considers it important to celebrate not only the birth of Christ, but also the *waiting* for the birth of Christ. Advent is meant to put us spiritually in touch with the longing for salvation, particularly of the Jewish people, that finds its fulfillment in Jesus. Advent points to the fact that the salvific event of Christ does not come "out of the blue," but is the culmination of an entire history of salvation in dialogue with God. It presupposes the idea that the coming of the Messiah, Christ, was the fulfillment of the expectations of the Jewish people, and had been promised and foretold by the prophets for centuries before his birth.

In the words that a French Christmas carol puts in the mouths of the shepherds at the Nativity, "for more than four thousand years the prophets have promised him to us . . ."[1] Most Christians no doubt understand this idea in a fairly straightforward way, without thinking too closely about the nature of the "promises" of the savior. We probably take it for granted that the Old Testament contains many texts— like those Handel gathered together and used as the basis for the first part of his most celebrated oratorio—that directly foretold the coming of "The Messiah," and that can be clearly seen to have been fulfilled in Jesus.

It is of course true that the Old Testament abounds in promises of God's salvation, often centered on a coming event or person. But the precise focus of that salvation changes greatly in the different periods of Jewish history. Even in the period immediately before the Christian era, the situation in Judaism was much more complex than we may at first imagine—as today's gospel shows.

The Jews did await a savior; but there was no consensus on the exact nature of that savior. Many people expected God to raise up a Messiah—the Lord's "anointed"—in the traditional sense of the term: that is, a King. He would come from the line of David, and as a political and military leader would restore the independence of Israel. Others, however, expected a priestly Messiah, a descendent of Aaron. Some looked to a prophetic figure "anointed" with God's spirit, as announced by the later writings in the book of Isaiah (first reading). Some (the Essenes, for example) seem to have expected several different "messianic" figures.

The hopes of yet others were not focused on a "messiah" at all. Rather, they awaited a direct intervention by God, anticipated by warnings from a prophet of the last days. Thus John is asked in the gospel: "Are you Elijah?"— the ancient prophet who was raised bodily to heaven, and who, according to tradition, was to return to announce the Day of the Lord, the eschaton. He is likewise asked, "Are you the prophet?"—that is, the "prophet like Moses," whom some Jews thought would come in the last days.

John denies that he is either the Messiah or any of the other anticipated figures. He is only a precursor; he prepares the way for the one who is to come. But then comes Jesus. Who is he, with regard to the expectations of Israel? Is he a political liberator? Elijah returned to earth? a new Moses? one of the prophets?[2] None of these ideas corresponds exactly with Jesus' true identity and function—even though there are elements in each that can be seen to be fulfilled by Jesus in a different way than anticipated. Even the title "Messiah" (or "Christ") is applied to Jesus in a sense that radically transforms the normal Jewish expectations.[3]

The "fulfillment" of the Jewish anticipations of salvation took place in Jesus in an unforeseen way: a way that challenged the expectations themselves, and was therefore unrecognizable or unacceptable to many. This does not lessen the parallel between the period of Old Testament preparation and our Advent. Indeed, in a certain sense, it deepens the connection: for it reminds us that even we who live after Jesus' life and message are celebrating and awaiting something that we cannot totally define or comprehend. In this sense also we can find a connection not only with the salvation history of the Jews, but also with the long "Advent" of the gentiles, the longings and fears for all humanity, seeking a final word of salvation from God. For we also have different visions of the Christ and the salvation he represents. What does Jesus mean to us? Is he a legislator and teacher of morality? a miracle-worker and giver of gifts? a mystical priest? What do we hope for from God? Protection and defense for our lives? good fortune and prosperity? a heavenly reward in the "hereafter"?

An important part of the message of Advent for us is that we must not restrict the coming of God with overly narrow ideas and desires, for if we do so, we risk not recognizing God's arrival. Jesus goes beyond his Jewish forebears' expectations—and also ours. The memory of Jesus orients our lives and defines our hopes. But it does not reduce the mystery of God or allow us to see clearly what God is as our future. For this reason Advent is not merely a memorial of a past stage of anticipation, but is a permanent condition of those who listen for God's word.

Nevertheless, we live in joy. Our first reading characterizes God's anointed as one "sent to bring glad tidings"; our responsorial psalm repeats Mary's words from Luke's gospel, "my soul rejoices in my God"; the second reading begins with St. Paul's admonition to "rejoice always." God remains mysterious, even after we receive his salvation; but we rejoice in that mystery, for it is revealed as the mystery of love. God does not simply correspond to our expectations or to our every desire; but God's word in Jesus and in the Spirit progressively *teaches* us what to long for. To wait for God's coming means to open ourselves to the always "more" of love.

NOTES

[1] "depuis plus de quatre mille ans, nous le promettaient les prophètes"—from the carol, "Il est né, le divin Enfant."

[2] See Mk 8:27–30 and parallels (Mt 16:13–20; Lk. 9:18–21), where various popular opinions about Jesus' identity are summarized.

[3] Even though there is still discussion of the meaning of the so-called "messianic secret" of the gospels (the fact that Jesus commands others not to speak of him as the Messiah—see for example Mk 8:30 and parallels, Mt 16:20; Lk 9:21), scholars are generally

agreed that there is no convincing evidence that Jesus claimed the title "Messiah" in any of its possible senses during his lifetime. It became a primary way of identifying him (among Gentile Christians even being used as his proper name, "Christ") after the resurrection; but the title as used by the church has been transformed and given its content by Jesus' ministry, passion, and death. The New Testament makes it clear that Jesus' "kingship" is of a different order from that generally associated with Jewish messianism of the period.

Third Sunday of Advent—Year C

Zep 3:14–18
Is 12:2–3, 4, 5–6
Phil 4:4–7
Lk 3:10–18

In 1886 the great novelist and thinker Leo Tolstoi wrote a penetrating analysis of the dire poverty and the glaring inequalities in his native Russia, calling attention to the injustice of the prevailing social system. He called his essay, "What ought we to do?"—the title being taken from the gospel passage we have read this morning, where the question is addressed to John the Baptizer.

Why did Tolstoi make this association? What similarity is there between recognizing contemporary social problems and awaiting the coming of the Messiah?

For Tolstoi, the need to do something about society arose precisely from the consciousness of God's presence in the world. It is possible, Tolstoi realized, for people to confront a problem in various ways. "The most terrible solution," he wrote, ". . . causes me to shudder. We could attempt to convince ourselves that the problem will right itself, and do nothing." It is the awareness of God—whether expressed as eschatological expectation (God is coming) for the Baptizer, or a personal crisis of conscience (God is present) for Tolstoi—that forces us first of all to acknowledge that there is a problem, and, even more importantly, to realize that we have to do something about it.

We are in the midst of Advent, anticipating Christmas: the feast of the presence of God in humanity. The contrast between its message of peace and the realities of everyday life that we read in the newspapers must inevitably and forcefully remind us of the problematic character of our world. It should also confront us with the realization that we must do something about it.

It is to help bring us to this realization that the church celebrates Advent—a season of expectation and preparation. Advent's deeper meaning is largely lost today, as the church's seasons become increasingly marginal to the secular contexts of our lives. Our preparations for Christmas are mostly external, and are focused on the celebration. We have many things to do: shopping, housecleaning, exchanging greetings, going to obligatory parties and social gatherings. Many preachers rightly remind us every year of the danger, in our situation, of missing the point. If we are to be touched by the celebration of the coming of God, if we are to make it an occasion to greet God in our lives, we need a very different sort of preparation: prayer, aloneness with God, the setting of priorities in our lives, opening our spirits and making room in ourselves for God's coming anew.

But in all this it is important that we not restrict our spiritual vision. Just as our material, societal preparations may lead us to miss the dimension of interior readiness, so an exclusive preoccupation with the individual and private dimension of spiritual preparation for God's coming could lead us to miss its wider implications.

The coming of God, as the Baptizer saw, is the coming of the cleansing fire of God's justice; it implies a need to change the world. When asked, "What ought we to do?" John indicates the need for justice toward others and the sharing of goods. Our preparation also means making our attitude like that of God coming to the world: a compassion which is also a cleansing fire. For the "coming" of God means that God does not merely remain a transcendent mystery, ever beyond, the subject of internal religious concern; but that God is relevant to the here-and-now world, and is therefore also the subject of social, political, and economic concern. It is also a concern that goes beyond the individual and personal, and involves us as a community in the question, "What must *we* do?"

In our second reading, St. Paul, reflecting on the nearness of the Lord's coming, tells the community of Christians to "rejoice in the Lord always"—and immediately afterward he says, "everyone should see how unselfish you are." There is a connection between the two: openness to others depends on interior, joyous communion with God; and conversely, our ability to rejoice in God depends on opening our concerns to God's, opening ourselves to loving those God loves. Superficially, it may not seem to be so. Poverty, homelessness, injustice, the problems of the world, are upsetting: they threaten to destroy our peace of mind, our sense of joy. Frequently, they make us anxious or angry. It would be easier and more pleasant to ignore them. But to do so would be to deny God's coming and the deeper joy it promises. Only if we are able to face the anxiety of heart that comes not from selfishness, but from concern for others, can we have real peace. Only when we ask the upsetting question, "what then shall we do?" can we attain to "God's own peace, which is beyond all understanding."

Fourth Sunday of Advent—Year A

Is 7:10–14
Ps 24:1–2, 3–4, 5–6
Rom 1:1–7
Mt 1:18–24

Today's liturgy shifts our attention rather abruptly from the general theme of God's "coming" into human history to the specific expectation of the birth of Jesus. The young woman Mary, heavy with her child, becomes the concrete image of our hope. It is an image that most of us can relate to readily and emotionally. Most of us as parents have experienced the joyous and nervous sense of hope that accompanies those last weeks of awaiting the birth of a child; all of us can be touched by the feeling of expectation, which is heightened by the knowledge that we also were once so tenderly carried and so eagerly awaited.

This sense of joyous expectation is a remarkable thing. We feel committed and vulnerable toward this new being even before it arrives, even though we do not know its face or its future. We do know that it will be a human life, a life like ours: full of ambiguity and risk, growth, questioning and sorrow. Yet despite all this, and despite the knowledge of the pain and self-sacrifice involved in being a parent, we await a birth with a sense of gift.

Expectant parents, in fact, often seem just like children awaiting Christmas; or rather, *vice-versa:* the anticipation that children feel of the joy of *receiving* material gifts is an analogy—at the level of which they are capable—of the anticipation of the much deeper joy of *giving* life, which is itself the anticipation of sharing in an ultimate level of *being* as gift.

What is the source of this joyous expectation, the radiance that surrounds a new birth—not only for the parents, but even for others? Is it only an emotional reaction built into us by nature as a reinforcement of our animal instinct to preserve the species? It would be foolish to deny that this is a part of it. But there is also a specifically human dimension that accompanies and builds upon our instinctive affirmation of new life. There is an implicit dimension of hope about the *meaningfulness* of life, despite all its ambiguity. To be able to find joy in loving, caring and giving unselfishly to a helpless child, prior to any merit on its part, and without the possibility of return, implies the hope—even if never made explicit—that this kind of gracious and unmerited love is in fact what human existence is about; and this hope can only have an ultimate grounding if reality itself is ultimately affirming and gracious; if its meaning is in the last analysis given by an ultimate reality whose nature *is* total and gratuitous self-giving, or love.

The message of the Advent season is that because of this eternal reality of self-giving love, which we call God, there is reason for *all*—the poor, the suffering, the aged, those who apparently have no worldly expectations—to live with the same excitement, anticipation, and hope as an expectant mother or a young child (one who has not yet learned greed) awaiting Christmas gifts. There is something good to come; the graciousness of being awaits us. The world is pregnant with an unknown gift of new life. Its birth, like every birth, implies a pain that is overshadowed by the joy of its promise. That new life is the continuing birth of Christ; not as a mere liturgical commemoration of a past event, but as a reality still ahead for each of us.

Jesus, of course, is not born again as a child. But there is another dimension to his "birth" to which St. Paul refers in our second reading. Paul speaks of Jesus as God's son in two parallel phrases: he was "born of the seed of David according to the flesh"; but "made Son of God in power according to the spirit of holiness, by his resurrection."

That is, the resurrection according to Paul is a new kind of birth for Jesus, the culmination of his birth, now as the Son of God in power. But the resurrection is not merely an event in past time; it is the event by which Jesus becomes present to all time, as the transforming power of love. In this sense, Christ's birth as God's son *in power*—in the power which gives life and grounds our hope—is still continuing; for each of us, it is still to come in its fulness, as we join that birth.

For each of us, then, the moment is pregnant: ready to bring forth the surprising gift of new life. If we are open to the spirit transforming us, we can live with excitement, anticipation, and joy; not merely as a seasonal mood, or a sentimental fiction, but as the real expression of the basis for our life, experienced within us.

Fourth Sunday of Advent—Year B

2 Sm 7:1–5, 8–11, 16
Ps 89:2–3, 4–5, 27, 29
Rom 16:25–27
Lk 1:26–38

This Sunday's gospel is a familiar one from its use by the church in the Marian feasts of the Annunciation (March 25) and the Immaculate Conception (December 8), and even more from the repetition of the angel's greeting in one of the most widely recited Catholic prayers, the "Hail Mary." Today's Advent use of the passage puts it in its original scriptural context, in which the principal focus is not on the bearer, but on the one who is to be born.

Specifically, the announcement is of the coming of the Messiah, the successor to the king David. The words of the angel to Mary are a purposeful echo of a passage for the second book of Samuel (part of which is used for our first reading), in which the prophet Nathan speaks to David concerning God's establishment of his royal house. When the passages are read together, the parallels between them are evident and striking. God says to David through the prophet, "I will make you famous" (literally, "I will give you a great name"), while the angel says of Jesus, "great will be his dignity." God tells David, "your house and your throne shall be firm forever before me and your throne will be stable forever"; the angel tells Mary, "the Lord will give him the throne of David his father, and he shall reign over the house of Jacob forever, and his reign will be without end." Of David's son, God promises, "I shall be his father, and he shall be my son";

of the child to be born of Mary, the angel says, "he will be called the son of the Most High."

The last phrase is particularly significant. We are used to thinking of the title "son of God" in connection with Christ's divinity. But in its original context, it refers not to Jesus' "nature," but to his function: Kingship. For the ancient Jews, the King on ascending the throne became metaphorically the "son" of God. The whole people of Israel was God's "child"; and the King, who was considered the representative and embodiment of the people, was the "son" of God in a special way. In both of our passages, we find an echo of Psalm 2, a coronation psalm, in which God says to the King: "You are my son, this day"—i.e., day of his accession to the throne—"I have begotten you." Similarly, in Psalm 89, our responsorial psalm, the King, the descendent of David, shall say to God, "You are my father."

For Luke, however, there is an important difference between Jesus and the Israelite Kings of old. Jesus does not become God's son at his accession to the throne (which in Jesus' case is not a worldly event, but his establishment as Lord at the resurrection); nor is he "adopted" by God when his spirit-filled messianic ministry begins. Rather, he is born as the son of God—a point which Luke makes by insisting that Jesus is conceived through the power of God's spirit.

Nevertheless, Luke wishes to emphasize continuity with the past, with the promises of God to the people of Israel. One point of connection is in the royal associations of the title "son of God": Jesus is in fact the promised King. Jesus is not something totally new, but is the fulfillment of God's promises: he is what was waited for and hoped for. God's salvation corresponds to the hopes and desires of God's people, because those hopes and desires are inspired: they come from God.

At the same time, it is clear that the hopes of Israel are

transformed by the actual event of salvation. Luke knew very well, when he wrote, that Jesus would never occupy the regal throne of David in Israel. His kingship is real, but is of a higher kind: it transforms the idea of reigning into one of service and self-sacrifice. (In the same way, his sonship is on a deeper and more intimate level: Jesus' whole life, from its beginnings and in its most profound reality, is that of God's child, one who lives by God's own "breath" or spirit of life.)

Luke's message contains important lessons for us. We also are awaiting, hoping: for many particular things, and for the one central thing that we symbolize in Christ and his kingdom. We believe that God inspires our desires and hopes. But we must expect that God will also transforms them. On the one hand, what God prepares for us is greater than we can imagine; on the other, we nevertheless know it, anticipate it, taste it, in the life God gives us now—and particularly in what we do here, in thanksgiving and communion, even in the midst of the ambiguities of life and of the world.

All of us are no doubt by this time in the last stages of preparation for Christmas. The gospel message tells us that to prepare ourselves for the coming of the Messiah—the King—is to remember and open ourselves to what the coming of Christ in history really meant: the revelation of God's kingdom as love. That love does not overwhelm the world with power, but changes it from within. It transforms our desires themselves to be like God's desire: the desire to give ourselves to each other—to the lost and suffering—in love.

Fourth Sunday of Advent—Year C

Mi 5:1–4
Ps 80: 2–3; 15–16; 18–19
Heb 10:5–10
Lk 1:39–45

For Roman Catholics, at least those of an older generation, the words of today's gospel are probably the most familiar and most repeated of the entire New Testament: for along
with the words of the angel at the Annunciation, they form
the first part (and until the Renaissance, formed the entir-
ety) of the beloved prayer "Hail Mary."

Hearing those words in their original gospel context adds
a great profundity to their meaning. They express a theme
found not merely in this passage, but throughout Luke's gospel: what makes Mary blessed is not simply the biological fact
of being Jesus' mother. What truly exalts Mary, according to
Luke, is not a special privilege that makes her separate and
different—like being a member of the royal family—but what
makes her similar to us: her discipleship, her responsiveness
to God's word.

Our gospel passage recalls lessons garnered from other
periods of Jesus' ministry: when a woman cries out, "blessed
is the womb that bore you"—a phrase closely reminiscent of
the words of Elizabeth—Jesus replies, "rather, blessed are
they that hear the word of God and keep it" (Lk 11:27–28).
When Jesus' mother and brothers are seeking to see him, he
says: "My mother and my brothers are those who hear the
word of God and do it" (Lk 8:21). For Luke, the source and
center of the "blessedness" of Mary is found in Elizabeth's

last words: "Blessed is she who trusted that the Lord's word would be fulfilled."

In Luke's gospel, Mary is presented as the model disciple: one who hears, trusts, and obeys God's word. She is the example of those who empty themselves: Luke's "poor" and humble. This perspective unites the gospel with today's other readings. In the first reading, we hear that Bethlehem, although a tiny, humble city, will yet be the origin of the Savior. In the second reading, from the letter to the Hebrews, we find the lesson applied to Christ himself: he comes to do God's will, to submit himself humbly to the Father's plan of salvation.

To see Mary's discipleship as the model for our own means recognizing that we also stand in poverty before God, and must hear and obey God's word. Such ideas no doubt strike a jarring note to our modern minds, accustomed as we are to thinking in terms of liberty, autonomy, and self-fulfillment. But God's word is not an arbitrary blueprint for life imposed from without; it is what we find by the responsible exercise of our minds and hearts. Obedience to God and human freedom are not opposed realities on the same level: we obey God by finding our true freedom, and vice-versa. Our poverty and obedience before God mean the recognition that what our hearts and minds desire, our very freedom and selfhood, must have a direction and goal that comes from outside our finite selves; only so can they have any real meaning at all. In this way, all discipleship necessarily connects with the message of the cross: we must lose our lives precisely in order to save them.

In the same way discipleship, as represented by the figure of Mary, connects also with message of resurrection: obedience to God is life and joy. This joy is at the very center of the Christian message—the "gospel" or "good news" in general—as well as at the center of today's gospel passage.

Earlier (Lk 1:15) Luke had told us that Elizabeth would bear a prophet; now her child begins to prophecy, by leaping for joy. Likewise, Mary's reaction to Elizabeth's proclamation about her faith is one of joy: "my spirit exults in God, my savior." From the very beginning, the proper reaction to Christ is joy, happiness, because God's will that he comes to proclaim is love, fullness, life.

Within a few days we will begin to exchange greetings of the coming season by wishing each other a "merry" Christmas. We do so rightly, for Christian hearts should be filled with a joy that we wish others to share. Ours should not be the artificial merriment, the frantic forgetfulness of realities of life that so frequently masquerades as the "Christmas spirit"; ours is rather the merriment of remembrance of Jesus's life, that shows us where true happiness lies; remembrance of the promise of God's love.

Our merriment is not a momentary escape from the sorrows of world, but allows itself to be touched by them, embraces them in hope and confidence. It is the merriment of hearts free of anxiety, not because we deceive selves that all is right, but because we are genuinely convinced that all will be right. For the Christian, happiness is sign of encounter with what is ultimately real. To paraphrase a saying of Pierre Teilhard de Chardin, joy is the state of those who have the courage to place the center of their lives outside themselves.

First Sunday of Lent—Year A

Gn 2:7–9; 3:1–7
Ps 51: 3–4, 5–6, 12–13, 14, 17
Rom 5:12–19
Mt 4:1–11

Orthodox Christian doctrine has always insisted vigorously on the fact, taken for granted by the gospels and unambiguously affirmed by the later writings of the New Testament, that Jesus was a true and complete human being. The letter to the Hebrews tells us explicitly that he was completely like us in all things, including being tempted to sin (Heb 2:17f.), and that he learned obedience to God through suffering (Heb 5:8).

When we hear today's narrative of the temptations of Christ, therefore, we should not assume that we are dealing with an account of a single isolate event in Jesus' life, undergone once and then finished forever. Rather, it is more natural to think that our gospel is a literary construct that summarizes the temptations that must have assailed Jesus throughout his life, and even to its end on the cross.

Matthew's version of the temptation story is a skillful literary creation. In a brief space it dramatically presents its theological theme: Jesus is the man who overcomes temptation and thus is able to serve as the instrument of salvation. The setting of the scene in the desert, the use of the number forty, and the explicit citations from the book of Deuteronomy all invite a comparison of Jesus with the people of Israel, tempted during the forty years in the desert after the flight from Egypt. But in contrast to the Israelites, Jesus is victorious in the trial.

Naturally, the temptations themselves, as recounted here, have a symbolic dimension that applies both to Jesus and to his followers. Bread is the basic sustainer of life; for Jesus to provide bread for himself by a miracle would be to refuse to depend radically on the Father's provident care. A very common form of religion is that which sees our relationship with God primarily as a means of giving us power over life, of providing for our own or others' needs and wants. The gospel reveals this as temptation, one that Jesus rejects throughout his life. In John's gospel we are told that after the miracle of the loaves, the people wanted to make Jesus king (Jn 6:15), but he fled from them. Likewise here, he rejects the temptation to use his spiritual gifts to attain earthly power. By contrast, Jesus' most fundamental nourishment must be God's word. God is not a means, but is the very goal of life itself. This is not to deny the need for bread, nor God's involvement in our welfare; but faith seeks first God's kingdom, and is confident that all else will follow from God's loving care (cf. Mt 6:31f). Jesus would teach his disciples to pray first, "Thy kingdom come . . . ," and then to ask for daily bread. He also must likewise live in dependence on the Father.

The second temptation also centers on a misunderstanding of how God's power works in the world. It is the religious temptation to ultra-supernaturalism: expecting God to intervene in extraordinary ways, to perform miracles, to provide "proofs"; above all, to protect us from danger and suffering. But to demand of God extraordinary signs, to center one's religion on miraculous deliverance, is to reject the human condition as the locus of God's love; it is to set one's own way above God's plan for salvation; it is to seek to avoid the cross. In the garden of Gethsemane, Jesus prays to be delivered from his impending passion; yet he accepts the Father's will. He is not supernaturally protected from suffering and death; yet he retains his trust in God.

Jesus' rejection of the third temptation—to worship something other than God, for the sake of worldly success and riches—also echoes themes pronounced throughout his ministry. He tells his disciples that they cannot serve two masters (Mt 6:24), and that their treasure must be in heaven (Mt 6:19ff). He emphasizes the danger of riches (Mt 19:23ff). True greatness, he proclaims, is in becoming like a child (Mt 18:1–5): that is, powerless, lowly, humble in the eyes of the world.

Jesus' response to the temptations is thus meant to be a model for us. Our first and second readings echo this idea. The reading from Genesis is a poetical narrative that intends to teach that death, evil, and the generally "fallen" condition of humanity do not spring from God's will, but from humanity itself: from our egotism and self-will. The juxtaposition of the temptation and disobedience of Adam and Eve with the temptation and obedience of Christ leads to the point made by St. Paul in the letter to the Romans: Jesus is the new Adam, who overturns the reign of sin and gives to humanity a new beginning. He is therefore the "type," the model, of the humanity to come, the humanity to which we are called: those who find life in God through service and love.

First Sunday of Lent—Year B

Gn 9:8–15
Ps 25:4–5; 6–7; 8–9
1 Pt 3:18–22
Mk 1:12–15

For people whose image of a desert was primarily formed by films like "Lawrence of Arabia," a sight of the deserts of the Holy Land comes as a surprise. There are of course on the Arabian peninsula and in North Africa the great romantic deserts of our imaginations: places of startling simplicity and stark beauty, oceans of pure flowing sand. But much of the Middle East consists of a different kind of desert: hard, rocky, dusty, barren country, a place of intense heat and cold, populated by vipers, insects, scorpions, and disease; a dry and inhospitable place, lacking the basic elements for human life. It is a place not adapted to human existence: a place of death.

It is this aspect of the desert that makes it the appropriate setting for Jesus' encounter with Satan. Unlike Matthew and Luke, Mark does not specify any content to the "test" that Jesus undergoes there. Moreover, for Mark the temptation in the desert is only a beginning: he understands that the battle between Jesus and Satan continues throughout Christ's ministry, and that his final triumph occurs only on the cross. In this sense, the "desert" experience continues throughout Jesus' life. Although the desert evokes it symbolically in a dramatic way, the struggle against evil has no special arena: its field is the whole of Jesus' existence.

There is however another aspect to the symbolism of

the desert. It is the place of encounter not only with the devil, but also with God. Its loneliness provides the occasion for silence and prayer (an important theme in Mark); it provides simplicity and peace. Mark tells us that Jesus was "with the wild beasts"—possibly an evocation of paradise before the fall—"and angels waited on him." Analogously, in the Jewish and Christian spiritual tradition, the desert often serves as the place of refuge from the banality and the harrying forces at work in everyday life; its elemental starkness makes it the locus of contact with more ultimate realities. The "desert" in this sense may not have the physical landscape of the Middle East or North Africa. It may perhaps be a rugged mountain like the La Verna of St. Francis or Mt. Athos of the Greek monks; or the expanse of the sea; or even a retreat of human construction.

While many people have the experience of the desert in its symbolic meaning—the spiritual barrenness, emptiness, danger, trials and temptations of life—in the contemporary world, there is little opportunity for us to have the second kind of "desert" experience, in either the literal or symbolic sense. We have few places of escape from the pace and attitudes of the world around us. It is not surprising, then, that for many people the church on Sunday morning becomes the closest thing to the desert retreat: a place of simplicity, stillness and repose, with sacred associations, where one may at last put aside the worries and busyness of life and reach a calmness of body and spirit. (Perhaps this is one reason why so many people seem to resist calls for active participation in the liturgy: they come to church seeking the solitude and interior peace that are the precondition for enthusiastic public, communal worship, but that they cannot find in their daily lives; so that they spend their time in church trying to attain the contemplative state of mind that should be the preparation for liturgy. When people come into church directly from the preoccupations and frustrations of life—perhaps ironically symbolized by the church parking lot itself—it is no wonder that they are unprepared even for active listening, let alone communal singing and praying.)

Our brief gospel has a second theme: after Jesus' desert experience, he takes up his mission of preaching the "good news" of God's reign, thus continuing both the battle against evil and his communion with God. In Mark's perspective, the desert implies also a return to the world: not only because it is there that the forces of evil are to be met and overcome, but even more because of the positive side of the experience: for there is no genuine encounter with God that does not lead us toward encounter with others as well. Hence the two symbolic aspects of the desert are intimately connected: for the full sense of finding and being with God must be a turning toward love, which includes the sharing of God's life with others; and this takes place in the struggle against the power of evil, the building of God's reign by the changing of the world.

This theme provides a unifying key to this morning's readings, so apparently diverse. The proclamation of Jesus is the message we hear as the cross is imprinted on our heads at the beginning of Lent: "repent and believe in the good news!" The good news is that God is for us, that God's love is overcoming the powers of evil. The church connects this message with baptism, symbolized by the "washing" of the world by the great flood and the covenant with Noah. As our second reading makes clear, the washing of baptism "is no removal of a physical stain, but the pledge to God of an irreproachable conscience": that is, by baptism we make a commitment to reform our lives and thus to believe in and share in God's power coming into the world. This means that the two aspects of the desert are inextricably united for us as well. Our religion cannot consist simply in retreating into the simplicity and beauty of the church, seeking communion with God; it must also be a return into the danger and barrenness of the world with a commitment to make the good news real.

First Sunday of Lent—Year C

Dt 26:4–10
Ps 91:1–2, 10–11, 12–13, 14–15
Rom 10:8–13
Lk 4:1–13

Many will no doubt remember the much publicized furor which erupted at the time of the release of Martin Scorsese's film "The Last Temptation of Christ," based on the novel by Nikos Kazantzakis. A good number of Christian religious leaders branded the film as blasphemous (for the most part, without having seen it); Catholic authorities condemned it; and for weeks small groups of protestors could be seen outside the theater in New York where it was showing, praying the rosary over a loudspeaker and distributing leaflets.

Whatever may have been the artistic and religious merit of the film, its primary thesis—that Jesus was capable of being tempted to evil, and that he actually was so tempted—is firmly rooted in the New Testament tradition. Today's gospel gives a dramatic account of Jesus' encounter with and victory over the spirit of evil in the wilderness at the very beginning of his public mission. It is significant, moreover, that the three temptations that occur here—to provide material bread, to seek power, and to work miraculous signs—recur in different contexts throughout all four gospel accounts of the ministry. Each in fact represents a misunderstanding of Jesus' Messiahship: a way in which people want or expect him to act, but which Jesus must reject in order to be faithful to his true mission. Some come to him to have their material needs fulfilled: "Truly I say to you, you are seeking me not because you have seen signs, but because you have eaten your fill of bread" (Jn 6:26, after the multiplication of the loaves). Some wish him to be a political leader: "Jesus realized that they were about to carry him away to make him King; so he fled once more to the mountain, all alone" (Jn 6:15). Some desire clear supernatural signs: "The Pharisees and Sadducees then came and, to put him to the test, asked for a sign from heaven. He replied . . . 'An evil and adulterous generation asks for a sign, and no sign shall be given it except the sign of Jonas'" (Mt 16:1–4).

In Kazantzakis's book, the last and greatest temptation of Christ occurs at the end of his life, on the cross. Although Kazantzakis's idea of what that temptation is reflects his own religious vision more than any historical or scriptural view of Jesus, the notion of the passion as Christ's last temptation or struggle with the devil does correspond to the New Testament perspective. Luke ends today's gospel passage with the ominous sentence: "When the devil had finished all this tempting he left him, *to await another opportunity.*" The gospels are agreed that the passion of Jesus is the hour of the "Prince of this world" (Jn 14:30) whom Jesus must once more—and now definitively—overcome. Although Luke does not see that struggle as taking place on the cross (he even omits Jesus' cry, "My God, my God, why have you abandoned me?" [Mt 27:46; Mk 15:34], replacing it with "Father, into your hands I deliver up my spirit" [Lk 23:46]), nevertheless he clearly alludes to it in the agony in the garden, in which Jesus struggles between his own desire and the Father's will. Twice in this scene Jesus admonishes his disciples to "pray, so that you may not enter into temptation" (Lk 22:40, 46)—showing that he felt himself and them surrounded by the same power of evil with which he battles in today's passage at the beginning of the ministry.

It is significant that all three temptations or misunderstandings of Jesus' mission involve a kind of "ultrasupernaturalism"—a desire for God to intervene in history in a "miraculous" way, fulfilling our needs, showing the divine presence, and ruling over the world. It is likewise significant that the ultimate defeat of the tempter is in the passion: God does not save us by triumphal intervention, but by the victory of a man's self-sacrificial love; not by miraculously satisfying our desire for well-being in the world, but by showing that our real well-being and our truest desire are only gained in self-abandonment to God.

We pray in the Lord's prayer, "lead us not into temptation." In the same prayer, we ask for God to provide for us exactly those things concerning which Jesus is tempted: bread, power, security. The difference between the temptation and the prayer is that we place these things in *God's* hands; we do not attempt to make them ours. "*Give* us this day our daily bread . . ."; "*Thy* Kingdom come"; "Deliver us from evil." For Jesus, the rejection of the devil's temptations resides in adoring God alone, and in finally abandoning himself to the Father in death. For us the same is true. We are to live in confident expectation of God's meeting our needs, of God's rule, of God's ever-present good will and care for us; we are therefore to resist the temptation of trying to manipulate God into serving us, and rather to see ourselves, as Jesus did, as already loved by God and (therefore) called to give ourselves totally in the service of love.

God does in fact give us bread, which is more than bread alone: the sacrament of self-giving; God does rule, in the mystery of hope; God does watch over and care for us, giving us the sign and experience of God's presence in the communion of love.

Second Sunday of Lent—Year A

Gn 12:1–4
Ps 33:4–5, 18–19, 20, 22
2 Tm 1:8–10
Mt 17:1–9

I recently came across an old photo of the interior of the church where I celebrate the eucharist on Sundays. Over the altar, which was then flush with the back wall, hung a large crucifix, depicting Christ suffering the agony of death. In the 1960s this church, like many others, was remodelled. The altar was moved away from the wall, and the old crucifix was replaced with an image of the resurrected Christ ascending in glory from the cross. It struck me that this change in images was symbolic of a shift in the spirituality of the church, one that has had significant repercussions for our understanding of the meaning of Lent.

Older Catholics will have a vivid memory of what Lent meant in the days prior to the liturgical reforms that followed the Second Vatican Council. There were strict rules of fasting and partial abstinence on every day but Sunday. It was taken for granted that aside from observing the universal fast, one would also voluntarily impose on oneself some personal form of penance and self-denial: frequently one would "give up" a particular pleasure for the duration of the season, or would engage in special devotions, or both.

Such practices were thought to have a self-evident value. Indeed, they did not belong only to Lent, but were part of a vision of the whole of Christian life as involving self-denial. "Bear your share of the hardship which the gospel entails," says our second reading; and it was widely preached and unquestioningly accepted in the Catholicism of my boyhood that living the "good news" must involve hardship. One must share in Christ's suffering in order later to join him in his glory. The crucifix was a fitting symbol for the spirit of Christian life.

For many, the *aggiornamento* of the Second Vatican Council brought about a kind of transfiguration of the image of Christ—and of Christianity. Biblical scholars and preachers rediscovered the message of the resurrection. Centrality was given to the glorified, triumphant Christ. Moreover, it was seen that there is an element of that glory in the life of the Christian as well, not merely in a hoped-for hereafter, but here and now. The ancient symbolism of baptism was recalled: we have already died with Christ and been raised with him, so that we are living the resurrected life. Preaching and catechesis widely emphasized a more joyous, positive Christianity, one that stressed the goodness of God's creation and did not think of life as (in the words of the "Salve Regina" recited at the end of every rosary) a "vale of tears."

This shift in Christian spirituality, to the extent that it has affected our lives, may lead us to wonder not only about the sense of Lent as a season, but also about the notions of sacrifice and penance in general. If Christ has triumphed, then why should we still be called on to "take a share of his suffering"? Of course, we realize that everyone will in fact suffer to some extent in life. But why should there be suffering freely accepted and even purposely adopted? Of course we must renounce what is evil and bad for us. But why should we renounce things that are good? Isn't it true that we praise God more by using God's gifts well than by giving them up; by becoming all that we can be rather than by cutting off avenues of experience; by joy rather than sorrow?

All this, I think, is true. It is also true that the "older" spirituality sometimes gave Christianity a morbid and negative cast, and was sometimes in danger of losing the "goodness" of the "good news" altogether.

But it is also possible for us to mistake the meaning of our participation in Christ's glory, and the danger of doing so is especially present in a society like ours that is self-absorbed and self-indulgent. Were we to make our religion simply an extension of these attitudes, it would lose precisely what makes it worth having. A religion of "cheap grace" (as one twentieth century theologian has called it), without self-sacrifice and without demands—a religion that merely affirms what we have and are—would be incapable of speaking to us of God or of the deeper reality of our selves. Our faith must give us a vision of something worth striving for: something better than what we have and are; something that makes it worth while to surrender our present existence—not only when it is sorrowful, but even when it is good.

In this sense, the vision of the resurrected Christ is a reason for embracing self-sacrifice, not for avoiding it. In today's gospel, Christ is transformed, and is seen by the disciples in the glory of God. But he (and they) must still come down the mountain, to continue his mission and to undergo passion and death. The transfiguration is an anticipatory vision of Christ's resurrection; but to get to the resurrection itself, he must continue through life and experience death. For the glorification of Jesus is not simply something that happens to him—a lucky event like winning the lottery; it is what he becomes by his total love of God, his total self-giving. It would be an error to think that we can share that glory without sharing the same attitude and being transformed in some way.

We have, by virtue of our baptism, entered into the life of the resurrection. But our baptismal transformation from death to life is not an event of the past; it is ongoing in our daily lives, celebrated again in every eucharist, completed only in the moment of our death. We have a share in Christ's glory already; but it is a glory that anticipates, like that of the transfiguration: the something better that we hope for transforms and glorifies the present, shows us what we are in process of becoming.

That something is the reality of ultimate love. It is this alone that should underlie and inform Christian penance and self-sacrifice. It is the ultimacy of love that makes it possible and necessary for us to practice discipline: to form the habit of giving up the lesser good for the sake of a greater, the narrower self for the sake of a wider; it is the ultimacy of love that makes it impossible for us to seek joy or meaning in life simply for ourselves, without connection with those who are in sorrow and pain.

To live by the vision of the transfigured Christ, to live with the anticipated joy of the resurrection as our spirit and motivation, is not a less demanding, an "easier" religion than that of externally dictated rules of fasting and self-denial. On the contrary, it means that we are the more responsible for our self-discipline and self-sacrifice. We are called to see and use the world (including ourselves) as God's gift in love. By our union in Christ's spirit, we become not merely the receivers of the gift, but givers also, not existing in ourselves alone, but with and for others. In this vision we can commit ourselves to self-sacrifice not in a spirit of grudging duty, but with the joy of those who love to give.

Second Sunday of Lent—Year B

Gn 22:1–2, 9, 10–13, 15–18
Ps 116: 10, 15, 16–17, 18–19
Rom 8:31–34
Mk 9:2–10

In the interpretation that is most obvious, at least to the modern reader, the story of the transfiguration appears to be the account of an event that happened to Jesus at a particular point in his life. The gospel seems to say that in a privileged moment, Jesus' physical substance was miraculously changed: his body was transformed, taking on a glorified form.

There is, however, another reading of this passage—a very ancient one, found in a number of the early Fathers of the church, and accepted as obvious in much of the church's tradition—according to which the transformation that took place did not occur in Jesus, but rather in the apostles who accompanied him onto the mountain. According to this interpretation of the story, Jesus was not changed at all. Rather, the disciples' manner of vision was altered, their eyes were opened, and in that moment they saw Jesus in his true nature—that is, they saw him for the first time as he really was always. Strictly speaking, in this way of thinking, it is not Jesus himself who is transformed, since he exists at every moment of his life in the divine glory. Only his appearance is affected; that is, others are able to perceive this reality, normally hidden from them.

St. Ephraem the Syrian, for example, in a homily on this passage, wishes his listeners to understand that the light that illumined Jesus came from within himself, not from any outside source. St. Leo the Great likewise teaches that in the transfiguration Christ did not acquire anything new, but merely "unveiled" ". . . the royal dignity that rightly belonged to the human nature He had assumed . . . which He now wished to make visible to these three men. For while they remained in the body they could never look upon and behold that unspeakable and inaccessible vision of the Divinity which is laid up for the clean of heart unto life everlasting."

St. Leo and St. Augustine agree in pointing out that the chosen witnesses are permitted to see not with their eyes, but with their souls. And they behold something that "earthly" people cannot see during this life: the glory of Christ that all of humanity will behold at the Last Judgment. Others of the Fathers (St. Ephraem and St. John Chrysostom, for example) emphasize that even in this access of vision the disciples do not see the full glory of Christ, but only what their weak human spirits are able to take in.

In this patristic interpretation, the gospel of the transfiguration is an "epiphany" story: an account of the sudden brilliant manifestation of the divine in the human world, giving people a glimpse of God's glory. Such stories are found in other traditions as well. In the great Hindu classic, the *Bhagavad-Gītā,* the eyes of Arjuna are opened to see momentarily an overwhelming vision of the cosmic form of God, hidden under the appearance of the human Krishna. In another story, Krishna's mother, suspecting her little boy of having eaten dirt, forces him to open his mouth, and sees within it the entire universe. Our gospel differs from such stories in its context and its ending: the disciples' vision is connected with Jesus' historical passion and subsequent glorification. In Hinduism, the human form of God's manifestations is typically regarded as being in some sense illusory, a mere appearance that veils the blinding glory beneath. Christian faith, on the other hand, insists upon the reality of Jesus' humanity: it is precisely in his being truly human, and most specifically through suffering his passion, that Jesus is revealed as God's beloved son, the manifestation of the divine light.

For many modern exegetes, the connection with the passion is the key to the meaning of the entire narrative. Historically, the transformation of the disciples' way of seeing—their recognition of who Jesus really was all along—took place not during his ministry, but after the resurrection; and his glorification depended upon Jesus' first fulfilling what is predicted in this passage: his suffering as God's obedient servant.

Its "epiphanic" quality is the reason for the adoption of the transfiguration passage as the gospel for this Sunday in Lent: the theme of light makes it an appropriate part of the catechesis of those preparing for baptism at Easter. What happens to the disciples on the mountain is a symbol of what takes place in us through conversion, the sharing in Jesus' death and resurrection symbolized by baptism: our spiritual eyes are opened, and we are able to see things as they really are. When this occurs, we can see the true beauty of life, the glory that we so frequently miss because our appreciation of what is other than ourselves is dulled by egotism. All of life can become an epiphany, a manifestation of God's glory.

But we must remember that the event of the transfiguration is closely connected with the prediction of Jesus' passion. Like the disciples, we must see and appropriate the events of Jesus' death and resurrection in order to experience the transfiguration. To see Jesus as he really is means seeing a love that is willing to give itself without reserve for others. If our vision of others and the world is to be transfigured, it must share in the same attitude of self-giving. As Antoine de St. Exupéry said, you see the other as he or she is, only when you love.

Second Sunday of Lent—Year C

Gn 15:5–12, 17–18
Ps 27:1, 7–8, 8–9, 13–14
Phil 3:17–4:1
Lk 9:28–36

In the middle of giving a recent lecture—a particularly interesting and informative one, I thought—my glance chanced upon a student seated toward the back of my rather large college class. I wasn't sure at first, since other students blocked the view; I thought charitably for a moment that perhaps he was bent studiously over his notebook. But a closer look confirmed my first impression: the young man's head was resting on his arm on the desk, and he was fast asleep.

Although I do not encourage the use of the classroom as a dormitory, I have to confess that, on a human level, I feel a certain empathy with my young student. I cannot recall ever falling asleep myself during a college class, even the dullest of them (and they were many); but I frequently felt like doing so. And I know that I have frequently missed much more important matters because not my body but my spirit was asleep. How many occasions of encounter, of love, of learning or of wonder have I missed because my attention was elsewhere or my mind was dull, unaware of the opportunity being offered?

Although I look back at such occasions with regret, I cannot be too surprised at my failure—at my falling asleep, so to speak, at just the moment of revelation. It happens to all of us; and, as a friend used to say when preaching on this gospel, we are in good company: it happened to Jesus' chosen disciples.

Luke alone among the evangelists tells us that while Jesus was being transfigured in prayer, those he had specially called to be with him on the mountain—Peter, John, and James—had fallen into a deep sleep. Can it be without significance that it is the same three who are invited to be with Jesus on the Mount of Olives on the vigil of his death, and that there also they fall asleep during Jesus' prayer? (Lk 22:39ff.) One has the suspicion that we are dealing here not with a merely factual coincidence, but with a message in symbolic form.

The passage we have heard today occurs in Luke immediately after Jesus' revelation that the Messiah must suffer (Lk 9:18–27) and that his disciples must share in his fate. Furthermore, the synoptics are all agreed that the followers of Jesus did not grasp, during his lifetime, what Jesus was really about; and in particular that they did not understand the message about his suffering. In Luke's account of the Transfiguration, the disciples awaken to a prevision of the glory of the resurrection; but they are asleep while Jesus communes with the heavenly figures about his "passage" (in Greek, ἔξοδος—"exodus")—an allusion backward to the Exodus event as well as forward to Jesus' journey to glory through suffering and death. (Indirectly, then, we may also see a connection with Christian baptism, a "passage" that is likened both to the passion and to the crossing of the Red Sea.)

The implied reference to the passion reminds us that there are in a sense two "transfigurations" of Christ. There is his transformation in glory, in which Christ appears in the super-human condition of union with God. This is the transfiguration that we are eager for; it is the basis of our hope, the center of our religion. Like the disciples, we are wide awake for this vision of Christ. But there is also another transfiguration. In his faithfulness to his mission, Christ is forced to take on a sub-human condition: he is transformed in the image of human misery, abandonment, suffering, alienation. This is a transfiguration we would frequently rather avoid seeing. Like the disciples in Luke, we are prone to fall asleep when Jesus' example of communion with God involves facing the difficult passage through death.

Do we not prefer to think of Jesus as being always in loving communion of mind and will with the Father—rather than as struggling to face and accept a horrible death he cannot avoid, if he is to be faithful? Do we not prefer to think of God as triumphant—as the almighty Power that rules and triumphs, and that therefore can and will help us— rather than as that mysterious Love that, strange as it may seem, is somehow powerless before human freedom, and must allow the dear Son to die abandoned on the cross before being raised to glory—and that therefore may save us in the same way?

Of course, for faith it is Easter that is the last word about Christ's transfiguration—not the cross: Christ's humanity raised up to glory, not debased and broken. But the twofold transfiguration continues after Easter: namely, in *our* humanity, the humanity of the extended "body" of Christ. Here, too, it is easy to be alert to Christ in his glorious manifestations. It is harder to stay awake in spirit, to pay attention, to his presence in the ongoing passion: in the homeless on the streets, the starving in Africa, the victims of corrupt political systems—all those who are transformed, by their own agency or by others', to a sub-human state, and who aspire not to glory, but merely to life on a basic human level. We would rather not see them, rather not think about them. Like the disciples, we are tempted to "sleep" through this part of the transfiguration—to dull our sensibilities, to let our minds find rest elsewhere.

In proposing this text to us at the beginning of Lent, the church offers us a vision of hope, reminding us, as Paul says, that the Lord "will give a new form to this lowly body of ours, and remake it according to the pattern of his glorified body." But we later disciples must be awake to the full implications of the vision of Christ's glory and our own. We who are invited to the Mount of Transfiguration are also invited to the Mount of Olives, and on both we are invited to share the *whole* communion of Jesus with his Father. We must be awake, then, to both the glory and the misery around us: to the wonderful possibilities of human life, and to its tragedies. And we must see the relation between the two. Anticipating Christ's glory, we embrace the journey by which it is achieved: the sharing in the passion of Christ and the passion of the world.

Third Sunday of Lent—Year A

Ex 17:3–7
Ps 95:1–2, 6–7, 8–9
Rom 5:1–2, 5–8
Jn 4:5–42

In recent news stories, much of the negative side of religion has been in evidence. Acts of terrorism are linked with Muslim fanatics; a group of cultists commits mass suicide after a bloody siege by police; a doctor who performed abortions is murdered by a man associated with a Christian fundamentalist movement. In the republics of the former Yugoslavia, ethnic tensions are exacerbated by religious differences: Serbian Orthodox and Croatian Catholics combat against each other and against Muslims. In addition, there are the continuing long-standing conflicts between Catholics and Protestants in northern Ireland; between Muslims and Hindus in India; between Hindus and Buddhists in Sri Lanka. One is tempted to agree with the famous saying of the Roman poet Lucretius: "*tantum religio potuit suadere malorum*": only religion has the power to sway people to so much evil.

It is notable, moreover, that in many of the instances named the form of religion involved may be called a type of "fundamentalism": faith that sets itself against the modern world; faith without reason, based on sheer authority or tradition; faith as a political force imposing itself on others.

But perhaps the conflicts arising out of religious fanaticism and intolerance are only the negative aspect of a wider phenomenon that also has a more positive side. It seems

91

clear that the contemporary world is undergoing a revival of interest in religion. And there are signs that this revival—despite its sometimes unfortunate embodiments—is connected with elements arising from genuine spiritual consciousness: disillusionment with secularism; shock at the moral depravity of permissive societies; the recognition of a need for more than can be offered by materialist consumer culture; the awakening—in the image of today's gospel—of a thirst for God.

It may seem obvious to religious people that a thirst for God is a good thing. But as a human desire this thirst can be profoundly ambiguous; if it is truly to lead toward God, it must be open to progress and purification, as the symbolism of our readings today shows.

In our first reading, the wandering Israelites are physically thirsty; they want water. God, miraculously providing it, meets their needs. But note that this incident of the people's calling out to God to assuage their thirst is not given to us as an example of faith; on the contrary, it becomes proverbial in the Scriptures as an example of sin. The Psalm exhorts us: "harden not your hearts as at Meribah,[1] as in the day of Massah[2] in the desert." It is an example of precisely what faith is *not*. The Israelites, we are told, "tested" God: that is, they did not believe in God's goodness and mystery, but insisted that God must meet their needs, on their terms. The "thirst" here is not really for God, but simply for water. From the scriptural point of view, this is hardness of heart. It symbolizes a sinful kind of religion that wishes to use God as a means to some other goal—physical, emotional, or psychological—that is the real object of our desire.

By contrast, the gospel presents us with an example of real faith, a thirst that progresses. The woman really recognizes Christ when she forgets her own material thirst—her initial interest—and allows a new thirst to emerge, a thirst for "living water" whose existence she had not even suspected. Her progressive insight parallels and symbolizes the process of conversion: a movement out of our world and our apparent needs, to the level of what we are really made for and thirsting for.

The story of the woman at the well is particularly suited to the catechumens preparing for baptism at Easter: it symbolizes the deepening of faith from our initial attraction, which may have many motivations, to our encounter with the living mystery of God. It is also a challenge for all Christians: do we have a religion of thirst or of satisfaction? A religion that claims to have all the answers, or one that involves us in ever deeper questions, more wonder and mystery? A religion that sees God as fulfilling our needs, or one that recognizes that God *is* what we desire?

NOTES

[1] The root "rib" signifies "quarrel."
[2] Meaning "testing."

Third Sunday of Lent—Year B

Ex 20:1–17
Ps 19:8, 9, 10, 11
1 Cor 1:22–25
Jn 2:13–25

This morning's responsorial psalm provides us with a good example of the positive aspect of spirituality based on God's law. Far from finding it burdensome, the Psalmist glorifies the Law: it refreshes the soul, makes the heart rejoice, gives light and health; it is more desirable than gold, sweeter than honey. Why? Because it reveals God's will and gives God's people practical wisdom, the right way of living, and the blessings that flow from it.

In our contemporary society, so far removed from the "covenant" context of ancient Israelite religion, there are probably nevertheless many people—and not only those who make "law and order" their primary social/political value—who would sympathize with the psalmist's frame of mind. In the light of the complexity of life, the confusion of values, the profusion of choices to be made, the many gray areas, wouldn't it be nice to have a clear set of rules, a simple and doable code to live by? A divine law: it would indicate infallibly just what our responsibilities are (and what their limits are); it would give us a sure basis for peace of mind. We could be safe in the security of having done right, fulfilled our duty. And do we not have such a law? A good many Christians seem to think so; time and again one hears the essence of Christianity described as "keeping the ten commandments."

But there are problems with identifying Christian life and spirit with the code that we heard in our first reading. In terms of positive morality toward our neighbor, there is nothing particularly "Christian"—or even uniquely Jewish—about the precepts found in the Decalogue. They summarize a code of "natural" morality found (albeit with different emphases) in nearly all civilizations, and even in many pre-civilized cultures. (The same basic principles are found, for example, in the Code of Hammurabi and other Near-Eastern law codes, upon which the biblical formulation is possibly based). Moreover, although the Bible extols the Law as a special gift of revelation from God, one can find similar ideas in ethical systems (like the Chinese) that find their basis simply in human reason. On the other hand, with regard to duties toward God, Christians do not follow those particulars of the Ten Commandments that are specifically connected with the Covenant of Israel and with Jewish ritual, like the prohibition of images and worship on the Sabbath.

In some ways the Ten Commandments, when seen in their context in Exodus, must seem to a twentieth century person a rather primitive and inadequate formulation of morality. They presuppose, for example, the legitimacy of slavery and of a patriarchal family system; in contrast to the ethics of Socrates or Confucius, they inculcate obedience on the basis of reward and punishment, rather than because of the intrinsic goodness of virtue; even while stating a moral code, they give an immoral example in their portrayal of the divinity, portraying God as unjustly inflicting punishment on children for their fathers' sins.

But the inadequacy of identifying Christian life with obedience to the Decalogue is based on a more profound reason than the time-conditioned character of the Exodus revelation. In Pauline terms, it is not "law," but "Spirit" that governs Christian life. Even a statement of the Ten Commandments that was altered and reformulated in terms of the "new covenant" would be insufficient. For the Christian, life and its decisions are not based on the security of the law, but on the risk of faith; not on a code, however valid, but on the person of Jesus and his example. In its root, Christian morality is based on the imitation of Christ's giving of his life for others. It does not allow us ever to be satisfied with having "done our duty," because it is based not on duty, but on love, which always uncovers further dimensions and always asks more.

The shift in mentality to a life based on the dynamic principle of the Spirit is symbolized in our gospel passage. The "cleansing of temple" by Jesus, at least as presented in John's gospel, is not to be thought of as a mere reformation of abuses, but rather as a prophetic gesture symbolizing something much more radical: namely, the end of the temple and its entire system of worship. According to this insight, we misunderstand the passage if we think that Jesus is just setting things right in God's house by clearing out misbehavers who have profaned it with secular activities like buying and selling. On the contrary: the sellers of animals and the money changers belonged in the temple; they were a part of its functioning, necessary for the fulfillment of the ritual sacrifices called for by the Law. By driving them out, Jesus is breaking with the law, not re-establishing it. He is saying in symbol what is expressed theologically in the second part of our gospel passage: that the true temple—the place where God is met—is not that made of stones, but is the resurrected body of Christ.

That body for Christians is a present reality of which we form a mystical part. And just as the true temple is the resurrected body of Christ, so the true worship of God takes place in the Spirit that animates that body and gathers us into it (as we state in our eucharistic prayer); so likewise the true living out of God's purpose for us consists in being open to the Spirit of love. What refreshes the soul, gives light to the eye, and rejoices the heart is not a law that can be stated once for all and obeyed to the letter—but is communion with that one body, in the one Spirit. Its hallmark is not the security of duty done, but participation in a love whose demands—and whose joys—never end.

Third Sunday of Lent—Year C

Ex 3:1–8, 13–15
Ps 103:1–2, 3–4, 6–7, 8, 11
1 Cor 10:1–6, 10–12
Lk 13:1–9

Among the daily newspaper reports of tragedies and disasters of all kinds, there is occasionally one that particularly grasps the imagination and draws one's attention. Perhaps it has to do with a situation you could imagine yourself being in; possibly something similar just missed happening to someone you know; or maybe you are simply struck by a sense of special horror in the incident. This occurred to me recently while reading a story of an airline accident. Shortly after takeoff, a part of the body of a jumbo jet suddenly ripped away, creating a gaping hole. Nine passengers were sucked out and plunged to death.

For many people, the story raised questions about the general safety of air travel and the specific problems of aging aircraft and inadequate inspections. But for some people— the families and friends of those who were sucked out of the plane to a horrifying death—the questions must have been much more personal: *Why* did this happen? Why was it *these* nine whose lives were suddenly and horribly ended, while three hundred others returned in safety? For those who believe in God, such questions take on an added dimension: How could God permit this? Why did God not show to these people the help and protection for which we constantly ask? What is the relationship of God, whom we call "All-mighty" and on whose providence we rely, to such a tragedy?

Put in this form, the question becomes universal. One could substitute any of the accidents and disasters that we hear about daily on the news or that we experience, perhaps less dramatically but no less profoundly, in our own lives.

The "news items" of Jesus' day, as we hear in today's gospel, were equally—or perhaps even more—filled with human tragedy. How does Jesus face the question about God's involvement in the ills that befall people?

Jesus does not give a systematic or philosophical response to the problem of God and evil. But by his actions, as well as his teachings, he seems clearly to reject one answer that was commonly held in his time: namely, that the disasters that befall people are to be seen as a punishment from God for their sins. By taking the side of the poor and suffering and declaring them dear to God, by curing people of illnesses, by preaching God's endless forgiveness and commanding that we imitate it, Jesus tells us that God is not punishing us through the evils that beset us, but is on our side in the struggle against them. In John's gospel, when the disciples articulate the traditional theological position that affliction is the result of sin, Jesus explicitly rejects it.[1]

Yet in today's gospel passage, Jesus uses the tragic events of his time as a warning: "You will all come to the same end unless you reform!" Furthermore he seems to imply, in the parable of the fig tree, that there is a limit to God's forbearance; the tree that does not bear fruit will be cut down.

The point of these sayings must be seen in the light of Jesus' reading of the signs of his times. Jesus believed that the end time was near; that the Kingdom of God was soon to arrive in glory, bringing first a time of tribulation, a historic crisis for God's people Israel. The verses immediately preceding our gospel passage speak precisely of the imminence of this time of crisis. In this light we can understand the urgency of Jesus' call to conversion and the sense of his warning. Those who suffered from Pilate's violence or from an everyday accident are not greater sinners who have been singled out for divine retribution; but their fate is an example of being caught unprepared by death and judgment: what will happen to all if they do not seize the opportunity to repent before the coming end times arrive. Jesus is telling his audience that *now* is the time of grace, before the axe is laid to the barren tree; there is still time to bear the fruit of repentance.

The "now" to which Jesus refers is also *our* time of grace. For the crisis for Israel, the eschatological time, did indeed come, although not in the expected way. Jesus experienced the eschatological time of trial in his own rejection and death on the cross; and Christian faith proclaims that through it he entered and brought about the Kingdom.

But the crisis for all of humanity was not completed in that single historical moment; it remains in the continually threatened future of human life, which still and always stands under the menace of tragedy and death. People do not suffer the tragic accidents of life because they have been bad. Both the teachings and the life of Jesus—in particular his cross and passion—tell us that God is not the source of this threat, but stands on our side in the struggle against evil.

But this insight has a disturbing logical consequence: if being bad is not the cause of suffering and tragedy, then being good is not going to prevent them. Evil can occur to those who love God and whom God loves just as well as to those who have rejected God.

God cannot create a world which is free and evolving and at the same time guarantee to preserve us from the accidents of life and the results of human choices—any more than the Father preserved his beloved son from the cross. God cannot secure our earthly future in and for itself. But the point is that life is not in and for itself; it is in and for

God. If Jesus' death teaches us that evils occur even to those who love God, his resurrection teaches us to hope in God's more ultimate triumph over evil. It teaches us, therefore, that the struggle for goodness, the struggle against evil of every kind, is not in vain, despite our apparent failures.

God cannot make for us a perfect and risk-free world; such a world would not be compatible with our freedom. What God can do, and does, is to offer continually the year of grace to the barren tree; to give to human freedom the possibility of finding meaning in life, despite its uncertainty and tragedies. That possibility lies in choosing to live for love. That year of grace is now.

NOTE

[1] John 9:2ff.: the curing of the man born blind. This passage is the gospel for the fourth Sunday of Lent, year A.

Fourth Sunday of Lent—Year A

1 Sm 16:1, 6–7, 10–13
Ps 23:1–3, 3–4, 5, 6
Eph 5:8–14
Jn 9:1–41

As my grandmother reached the end of her long life, she began to lose her sight. Her blindness went through progressively worsening stages until, at the end, she could only recognize the strongest contrasts of light and dark.

A parallel process took place in her mind. As she lost her sight, she increasingly lost contact with the present world around her, and began to live more in a totally private world of memory, fantasy, and imagination. She frequently could not remember where she was, and fancied that she was in the home of her youth; she often could not distinguish between what had happened in her dreams and what was actual. The things that were most important to her remained clear: she recognized her family and her relationship to them and even the current details of their lives. But all the rest—time and place and circumstance—became as blurred and indistinct as her vision.

Our gospel presents us with a similar parallel between physical sight and mind. Sight is used here symbolically as a metaphor concerning insight, which in regard to spiritual reality is faith. A popular saying tells us that "seeing is believing." In John's gospel, on the contrary, it is believing which is (real) seeing. Faith, that is, is a kind of "sight," a way of encountering and knowing reality beyond the merely empirical. The story in today's gospel tells of the process of gaining this sight—coming to faith—and of going blind—losing contact with what is ultimately real.

The blind man in the story both gains his physical sight and comes to spiritual insight about Jesus. He comes to see physically in a single symbolic gesture of washing; but this is only the beginning of his progression in coming to faith. At first he identifies his healer simply as "the man they call Jesus" (v. 11). Then he acknowledges him as "a prophet" (v. 17). Still later he claims that Jesus must be "from God" (v. 33). And at last his spiritual eyes are fully opened in the final encounter with Jesus, who reveals himself as "the Son of Man" who is the object of faith (v. 37).

At the same time, the Pharisees grow progressively blinder. Initially, they are open to the fact of the blind man's miraculous healing; but subsequently their minds begin to close: they begin to doubt the man, and call upon his parents; then they attempt to trap him in his repetition of the story; in frustration and anger they vilify the witness and throw him out; and finally, their bad will and refusal to believe are judged by Jesus and exposed as spiritual blindness.

The key to the passage is found in Jesus' solemn pronouncement:

"I came into this world to divide it,
to make the sightless see
and the seeing blind."

The saying may initially be disconcerting: Jesus apparently claims to have come not only in order to bring sight, but also to cause blindness. But the notion that Jesus' mission is to bring division and to set people at odds is familiar from the synoptics (see for example Mt 10:34ff. and its parallel, Lk 12:51ff.); and our passage is to be interpreted in the same way. Jesus brings a crisis of decision: he forces people to make a choice for or against what he represents—God's saving action in history. For John, Jesus himself is the light: one must either accept its presence and see clearly, or turn away from it into darkness, becoming blind. For this reason Jesus holds the Pharisees responsible for their blindness (v. 41).

The church traditionally connects this passage with baptism. The blind man's washing, which brings sight and begins the process that culminates in acknowledging Jesus, symbolizes the sacrament of initiation into the faith community. This gospel reading was especially appropriate for Lent, during which catechumens were prepared for baptism at the Easter Vigil (a practice now restored in the Rite of Christian Initiation for Adults): their eyes are to be opened to a new vision of faith through their decision to respond to Christ, the light.

For those who are long-standing members of the community, particularly those who were baptized as infants and received its teachings as a part of their familial heritage, the emphasis on human choice in the conclusion of the gospel passage is an important reminder. Being a Christian is essentially a matter of making a free decision for faith in Jesus and all that it implies. It means choosing to "see" spiritually: to judge things in the light of Jesus' example and teaching.

Frequently people's spiritual and moral vision can be like my aged grandmother's declining physical vision: just as her failing eyes could distinguish only the strongest contrasts of light and dark, so for the spiritually blind most of life appears as a shadowy gray area, where only the strongest contrasts between good and evil can be discerned. Few of us would consciously choose darkness instead of light; but we end up choosing the darkness *along with* the light, for we lack the insight to distinguish clearly between them. Just as my grandmother's physical blindness detached her from reality and led her to live in a world of imagination, so when our spiritual vision is unclear we live not in the world of real value, but in a fantasy world of our own construction.

But our gospel reminds us that unlike physical sight, spiritual insight is something about which we have a choice and for which we are responsible. We are still in the process symbolized by the story of the blind man: gaining the vision that began when we entered the faith community in the washing of baptism, learning just who the Son of Man is and how we are to relate to him. But Christ has already opened our eyes, and calls us to progress in our vision by choosing to live our lives by our faith. As our second reading tells us, "once you were darkness, but now you are light in the Lord; live as children of the light." Lent is for us an invitation to renew our decision to see clearly: that is, to live by the "light" of faith that we have been given: the presence of the divine love in our hearts. That love is the presence of the risen life in us. It gives us the courage to discern what is real and valuable, to distinguish good from evil, to separate the works of light from those of darkness—to be correct, as St. Paul says, in our judgment of what pleases the Lord, and to produce "every kind of goodness and justice and truth."

Fourth Sunday of Lent—Year B

2 Chr 36:14–17, 19–23
Ps 137:1–2, 3, 4–5, 6
Eph 2:4–10
Jn 3:14–21

One of the events that has most excited the art world in recent years was the completion of the cleaning of the great fresco series in the Sistine Chapel in Rome. These masterpieces, their forms long darkened by a film of soot and dirt, are now revealed in brilliant color. The final and most controversial work of the project was the restoration of Michelangelo's great portrayal of the Last Judgment, which by its monumental size and position dominates the entire chapel.

This gigantic mural is clearly one of the best known works of art of the Western world. Thousands have stood before it and have been overwhelmed by its power. Even those who have seen it only in reproductions can be moved by it. Yet probably very few who feel the beauty of the art have any clear awareness of its message. Certainly, everyone can recognize it as a representation of the final judgment of the world. But probably not many advert to the disconcerting pessimism of Michelangelo's vision of that event, although it is symbolized clearly in the painting. Below the figure of Christ are portrayed two angels, each holding an open book. The one on the left bears the book of life, containing the names of the saved: it is a slim volume. The one on the right shows the book of death, naming those whose sentence is damnation: it is an enormous tome. The attitude of the massive figure of Christ is that of an angry judge, who

106

turns in wrath toward the evildoers being dragged down to hell. The scene might be an illustration of many a medieval sermon, like this typical one from St. Anselm of Canterbury:

> The day of judgment is coming . . . that great day of the Lord is nigh, it is near . . . the day of wrath and day of mourning . . . Barren tree, where is your fruit? You deserve to be cut down and burnt, cut up and put on the fire . . . Perhaps you think of some sin as small? Would that the strict judge would regard any sin as small . . .

Like most Christians of the Middle Ages and even afterward, Michelangelo took it for granted that the great mass of humans would be lost; that salvation was for the few; and that the main point of the Last Judgment would be the horror dawning for (in the words of a latter, literary portrayal by Jonathan Edwards) "sinners in the hands of an angry God."

We might well ask ourselves what the origin is of this emphasis on "fire and brimstone," this image of a fearsome God, this pessimism about human salvation—all so prevalent in the Christian tradition. Certainly, the New Testament contains stern prophetic warnings for those who "love darkness rather than light." But the essential message of Jesus is one of confidence, not of fear; the gospel is "good news." We are given in today's reading the ultimate sign of hope: "God so loved the world that he gave his only Son . . ." "God did not send the Son into the world to condemn the world, but that the world might be saved through him."

Why, then, is the image of a stern and vengeful Judge so common? Perhaps, on one level, it is the result of our projection: we make a God in our own image, one whose "justice" corresponds to our guilt and desire, anger and fear. When the "bad guys" in a film are violently blown away by the hero or heroine, do we not feel a surge of adrenalin, a satisfied feeling of rightness, even if our minds reject it? Certainly many people must, or such films would not be so popular. Do we unconsciously make God's justice a copy of our desire to destroy utterly whatever threatens or violates us? Humans seem to have a tendency to think of justice as revenge—as the balancing of some cosmic scale on which wrongdoers must experience an evil equal to what they have committed. (Recent outcries in favor of capital punishment, despite the lack of evidence that it prevents crime, seem to bespeak such an attitude.) Do we project this onto God? Perhaps there is even an explicit feeling that we need a God who punishes in order to protect the moral order: that a lack of standards goes along with a lack of sanctions. I have heard Christians voice the opinion that the preaching of the God of love goes along with permissiveness, and that the "fear of God" must be instilled in people to make them behave.

In a certain sense, God as the sternly just Judge is also easier to deal with—at least for those who think of themselves as being on the right side of the law. Salvation can be won, accomplished, by right conduct, obedience, performing the demanded rituals. One can have a "right" to it. It is much more difficult to deal with the idea of salvation proclaimed by Paul: "It is owing to God's favor that salvation is yours through faith. This is not your doing; it is God's gift. Neither is it a reward for anything you have accomplished" (second reading). This view means abandoning any attempt at self-justification, and recognizing that even in our freest, most personal decisions for goodness, "we are truly God's handiwork."

The creation of a God in our image of justice allows us to escape from the real challenge of the gospel: that God is love, absolute and unconditional. The presence of such love in the world does not do away with judgment. John's gospel, which most clearly proclaims the message of God as love, is also the clearest on the radical division of good from evil and on the reality of judgment. But it is a judgment that we ourselves perform. The Son does not come to judge—but judgment takes place. The presence of God's love manifest in Jesus provokes people to "judge" themselves by deciding for or against him, by living in the "light" of love or by preferring the darkness. The God of love thus demands more than the God of "justice," and demands something different: that we imitate God by becoming unconditionally loving. This means, in Paul's terms, basing our lives on faith: on the trusting acceptance of the unmerited gift of being loved by God. It is this which enables us to lead "the life of good deeds" (second reading) that are truly "done in God" (gospel) because they are not "ours," but the manifestation of God's gift in us. And because we experience that gift and its results as a pure, unmerited grace in ourselves, we can and must believe that it is likewise given and received in others, and that the "last judgment"—which is in the process of being realized now—will be the victory not of darkness but of light.

Fourth Sunday of Lent—Year C

Jos 5:9, 10–12
Ps 34:2–3, 4–5, 6–7
2 Cor 5:17–21
Lk 15:1–3, 11–32

In what is probably the most influential of all the Buddhist scriptures, the so-called *Lotus Sûtra* (probably completed some time early in the Christian era), there occurs a story that has a remarkable similarity to the passage from Luke's gospel that we have heard today. Frequently called the "Buddhist parable of the prodigal son," this story, like ours, tells of a young man who leaves his father and journeys to a distant country, where he becomes poor and miserable. But the subsequent unfolding of the story reveals a somewhat different perspective from that of the gospel.

In the Buddhist story, the father goes in search of his son, and spends many years seeking him. Finally the two encounter, by chance, and the joyous father hastens to reclaim his beloved son. But in the intervening years the father has grown so much older and so much more powerful and magnificent that the miserable son cannot recognize him, and will not believe that this is in fact his father; he is terrified of the rich and princely man, and flees. And so the father must in sorrow let him go again. But he sends messengers after him, and has them hire him to work in a menial position in his house. Then the father himself puts off his magnificent clothes and pretends to be a servant; and over the course of many more years, he gains his son's confidence and affection, so that he finally is able to say to him: "You must look upon me as though I were your own father." Only at the very end of his life is he finally able to announce that this is indeed his very son, to whom all his riches now belong.

The Buddhist parable has, of course, a very different religious context from ours. Nevertheless, we may find in it a psychological insight which complements that of our gospel. We are told constantly that God is our Father, that he forgives us, that he loves us, that he seeks us eagerly; but do we really believe it? In Luke's story, the returned son is willing to be a mere servant in his father's house, but when he is welcomed, he immediately enters into his rightful position and shares the Father's joy. How many of us are not more like the Buddhist son, who cannot accept himself as the child of such a father, cannot credit such wondrous love, and therefore remains for years as a servant?

There is a film of Ingmar Bergman's in which a character says of his wife: "I wanted to tell her that she is loved completely; but I couldn't find a way of saying it that she would understand."

There are people who have a strong—perhaps childish and naive—sense of their own worth, who take it for granted that they deserve to be loved. But the more maturely and realistically we face what we are, the more we realize our finitude; the more we recognize that we cannot justify an unqualified affirmation, an unconditional love. The more incomprehensible, then, becomes the message that we are in fact loved in just such a way. It can only be grasped by an attitude of complete openness; one that has ceased to attempt to justify oneself, and has accepted the astonishing fact of love as an unmerited gift.

It is not easy to accept such a message; we must hear it over and over. We must see it concretely in the self-giving love of Christ and of those who have loved us in imitation of his love. We must open ourselves to astonishment and humility and an overwhelming gratitude in order to receive it.

Once we have grasped—or allowed ourselves to be grasped by—the wonder of God's free affirmation, every attempt to gain affirmation of ourselves by having things, or by the control and manipulation of others (to which so many of our efforts are aimed!) is revealed as futile and pitiful. When we know and admit in humility that we are loved completely, then we are freed to love each other; liberated from envy and resentment, we can give to each person the free and generous affirmation that we receive in the core of our being from God.

Fifth Sunday of Lent—Year A

Ez 37:12–14
Ps 130:1–2, 3–4, 5–6, 7–8
Rom 8:8–11
Jn 11:1–45

On this last Sunday before the beginning of the liturgical drama that commemorates the culmination of Christ's life, our readings engage us in a reflection on resurrection, the goal of our entire Lenten journey of incorporation into the passion and death of Jesus.

In the passage from Ezekiel, which concludes the famous vision of the dry bones brought back to life by God's spirit, the idea of "resurrection" is used as a metaphor. Ezekiel's prophecy is not directly concerned with life after death, but with the salvation of God's people from captivity and exile. In Babylon, far from the land of the covenant, they are without spirit; it is like being dead. Their return to the land of Israel will be like a new life arising from the grave; God's spirit, the breath of life, will once more be in them. The focus is thus on an earthly "resurrection" by God's power acting in the world.

In our reading from Paul's letter to the Romans, the notion of resurrection takes on a new dimension. Here also, the primary focus is on life in the world. But this life, for Christians, is transformed by its sharing in the resurrection of Christ from the dead. To live, for the Christian, is to live according to what God has done for Christ. It is therefore a matter of living in the world not according to the "flesh," that is, self-centered existence, but according to the Spirit of God, who gave to Jesus new life out of death. Paul's reflection tells us that the human being cannot be happy or really alive when turned in to self; we must die to self and be resurrected in order to live in Christ by the Spirit, even now in our "mortal" bodies.

Our gospel passage speaks of the source of resurrected life: faith in Jesus. The story of the raising of Lazarus is not simply a demonstration of the power of Christ, nor a mere symbol and example of the resurrection of Christians (although it is also these): it is a lesson in the meaning of faith, which is the foundation of our new life. The purpose here is not to record a historical event as accurately as possible, but to challenge us to faith by giving an example of what faith is: we are to discover in our lives events that correspond to what happens in the gospel, and pattern our response on that of Jesus' earliest disciples. The symbolic dimension is particularly prominent in John's gospel. In today's passage, Lazarus and his sisters are presented as people Jesus loved, and hence represent Christians faced with the dilemma of death and at the same time confiding in Christ's life-giving power.

The story proceeds in a typical Johannine manner from one level of faith in Christ to another, deeper level, through a revelatory encounter with him. It begins with a limited understanding of and confidence in Jesus: incipient faith grasps Jesus on our terms, as a function of our needs. It moves, however, toward true faith: an acceptance of Jesus on his own terms, as the revelation of the real goal of life. This story is thus relevant especially to the process of the Rite of Christian Initiation for Adults, the catechesis now being undergone by those aspiring to baptism at Easter; but it also symbolizes the continuing call to a deepening of faith in each individual and in the entire Christian community.

The lesson in faith is artfully constructed. At a first level, both Martha and Mary express confidence in Jesus' power as a healer: "if you had been here, my brother would never have died." But this very faith raises a question: if Jesus loved his friend, and had power to heal him, then why did he let him die? The resolution is found in a new understanding of Jesus and a correspondingly new dimension of faith in him: Jesus does not merely cure, but raises from the dead. He is not merely a means to preserve life; he is himself "life" in its final dimension, that of the resurrection.

The faith that corresponds to this revelation has two important aspects. First, it must be ready to accept suffering and death. Jesus does not save his friends from these. Yet, even in the perplexity and sorrow of loss, there is confidence in his love.

Second, faith moves us beyond ourselves. It draws us out of our world, defined by our desires and needs, and puts us in the real world, which is God's. Concretely, this means that faith is ready to accept surprises. God does not simply correspond to our human expectations, but leads us through them to something always more. The center of our faith is summarized in the assertion not merely that God loves us, but that God is love. This means that what "love" is must be learned from God. Our idea of "love" must not simply be patterned on ourselves and our incomplete way of loving. Faith in God's love must leave room for growth and for surprises; it must have a sense of humor; it must be prepared to face the perplexity of accepting things that seem (and sometimes are) contradictory, like God's love and the experience of evil. To "believe in" Christ moves us out of the area of self-confidence and self-reliance into a position of exposure and risk: the position that results from making ourselves open and vulnerable to a personal relation. It is from this kind of belief that true life stems: "I am the resurrection and the life . . ."

The theology of the Johannine scriptures explicitly connects acceptance of this life of resurrection with the sharing in Christ's body and blood. What is here attributed to faith, is elsewhere said of the eucharist: "whoever eats my flesh and drinks my blood has eternal life, and I will raise him up . . ." (Jn 6:54). The eucharist is the sacrament of life and of the resurrection because it epitomizes the Christian act of faith: eucharist means acknowledging and receiving Christ as our food—that is, as the source of our life and growth. To receive it genuinely is to accept Christ in faith, on his terms: in transcendent mystery and in community with one another.

Fifth Sunday of Lent—Year B

Jer 31:31–34
Ps 51:3–4, 12–13, 14–15
Heb 5:7–9
Jn 12:20–33

In the period following the Exile, Jewish religious life eventually became increasingly focused on the Law. Authority began to be centered on scholars and teachers of the Law—the "rabbis" of later Judaism—rather than on the kings, priests, and inspired prophets who dominated earlier periods of Israelite history; indeed, the Judaism that began to evolve in the years of the Exile and developed in the post-Christian era continues to this day in a form frequently described by scholars as "rabbinic Judaism." A primary feature of the rabbinic form of religion was always its emphasis on learning (a trait which, as has frequently been noted, has carried over into a general respect for education among the Jewish people). The Covenant with God was considered to be mediated by the historical revelation contained in the Torah. In order to be faithful to the Covenant relation, God's people had to sanctify their lives by obeying the revealed Law scrupulously and generously in all things. But in order to obey, they had to know the Law and its meaning, and had to be able to apply it. Hence there arose over the centuries an immense body of commentary and rabbinic teaching, which explained the obligations of the Law, expanded upon them, and attempted to apply them to all circumstances. The study of these teachings, gathered in the multi-volumed Talmud, still occupies an important role in the lives of pious Jews.

In contrast to the rabbinic emphasis on continual study of the Law and scholarly debate on its meaning stands our reading from Jeremiah. The prophet foretells a day when there will be a new covenant: the law will be within, written upon the people's hearts; there will be no need for teaching in order for people to know God, for all will know the Lord directly. The time of mediation by external commands and by the word of others will be over; there will be direct, immediate experience of God.

Christians claim that the new and definitive covenant has come, in Christ, and that the final time announced by Jeremiah—even though its fullness still remains future—has been begun by the giving of God's Spirit.

If taken in all earnestness, the Christian affirmation is a remarkable one: it claims not merely that we have a new and higher set of laws, or even that we are in a new legal situation (where for example, our transgressions are no longer held against us), but that we have a new kind of being, a new relationship to God that goes beyond the mediation of any external law or teaching, even though these remain a necessary part of our lives. The Christian doctrine of the Spirit means that we have the life of God's self in us; not simply that we have divine help in living our human life, but that we are involved in a new form of life, a new level of being. The principle of this higher form of life is within us: we are to live by an immediate contact with God, with the invisible, ungraspable, eternal and transcendent. God's own being, in us, is the fundamental principle that interprets and judges all its external revelations and mediations.

But the presence of God's Spirit in us and the call to share in divine life even while we are living in the world creates tension within us, precisely because the process is underway and is not yet complete. In a sense, we are invited (as Teilhard de Chardin formulated it) to a new step in evolution. But to take that step, to become a new sort of being, to live on another level, also means a kind of death: "unless the grain of wheat falls to the earth and dies, it remains just a grain of wheat . . ." To enter the divine life means leaving behind the life that is bounded by the world and its sensations, the life that is natural to our animal and even our rational selves.

The tension that is present whenever growth occurs or a boundary is overcome is particularly acute here: for unlike the unconscious evolution of species, this step into the divine requires our collaboration, and hence comports a consciousness of the sacrifice that the progression requires. We must freely decide to give ourselves to the new life, and to renounce the old; to surrender what is for the sake of what can be. "The person who loves his life loses it, while the one who hates his life in this world preserves it to life eternal."

The prospect of any step into the unknown can bring fear, sometimes terror; all the more so when the unknown is the absolutely transcendent God, and the step into the new life involves anticipating our real physical death and making its inevitable sacrifice a part of our present existence.

The tension brought about by the immediacy to God's life is seen in two quite different perspectives in our readings. In our gospel, from John, Jesus feels "troubled" in spirit; but he will not pray to be saved from his "hour." There is no account of the agony in the garden in John's gospel. The passion for John is the hour of Jesus' "glory": it is seen from the perspective of the resurrection, the new life that comes from death.

In our reading from Hebrews, on the other hand, we are told that Jesus "offered prayers and supplications with loud cries and tears to God"; and that "son though he was, he learned obedience from what he suffered . . ." Perhaps most surprisingly, the letter continues: "when *perfected,* he became the source of eternal salvation." Hebrews emphasizes the negative, fearful aspect of Christ's passion, and sees it as part of a necessary process which Jesus had to undergo in order to attain perfection.

The Christian also can expect to experience the tension between dying and rising in our attempt to come to completion in God's life. On the one hand, we have confidence in God's love as our absolute future, from which nothing can divide us; on the other, the real evil of pain and death is not removed by the fact that it leads to an ultimate good. Hence our bodies and minds rebel against suffering, even when we have faith. A friend of mine who knew she would shortly be facing very difficult times expressed the situation with self-knowledge and humor. She said: "I'm not afraid of suffering. I have suffered before, and I've grown through it. I know it will be good for me. It's only when I'm facing it that I have a problem." Looked at from the end—from what it will produce, once it is over—the cross can be accepted; but when we are in its shadow, we tremble.

Living the Christian life, then, is a matter of hope: believing in and acting in accord with the immediacy of God. It means being conscious of, believing in, and valuing the future that we are on the way to becoming to such an extent that we can let go of all else. We experience God's immediacy as the "more" of existence that calls for generosity, love, and self-giving. The message of the gospel is that we are able to live by that "more," to "lose" our life in order to gain it, to face the realities of the cross, of suffering, of death. We are able to live with a courage and confidence whose reason is "beyond" us, because God is at the same time not merely beyond us as a future hope, but is present as the deepest reality in us.

Fifth Sunday of Lent—Year C

Is 43:16–21
Ps 126:1–2, 2–3; 4–5, 6
Phil 3:8–14
Jn 8:1–11

Several years ago the Western world was shocked by pictures secretly taken and smuggled out of Saudi Arabia showing the beheading of a young princess who had been found guilty of adultery. Since the rise of Moslem fundamentalism, especially in Iran, we have seen other examples of the application of Islamic law to offenses against public morality, including the flogging of "immodest" women and other severe punishments—including the death sentence—for immoral behavior, even in what we would consider "private" life. One of the most celebrated cases was that of Salman Rushdie, condemned to death for the crimes of apostasy and blasphemy because of his book *The Satanic Verses.*

While our modern sensibilities may be perplexed by such ideas of justice, today's gospel is a reminder that they are by no means foreign to our own Judeo-Christian religious tradition. The Law of Moses laid down the punishment of death for the crime of adultery (Lv 20:10); also for cursing one's father or mother (Lv 20:9), for fortune-telling (Lv 20:27), for idolatry (Dt 13:11), and for blasphemy (Lv 24:15). It was taken for granted during the Christian middle ages that intellectual dissent from the faith (i.e., heresy) should be punishable by death. It is only comparatively recently, in the wake of Enlightenment, that Western society has come to think of private morality and personal freedom as separable from rigidly imposed community norms. Through most of our Western and Christian history it has been presumed that there is no such thing as "private" morality; that error has no rights; and that the community as a whole must protect itself from deviations from its norms by cutting off the offender—the same presumptions that motivate the prescriptions of Islamic law.

Indeed, the basic attitude behind such ideas is one which we can find widespread within contemporary society and perhaps even within ourselves. Do we not all feel *outrage* at certain crimes, and feel that their perpetrators "deserve" punishment? Do we not feel a surge of righteous anger when we hear of a drug-dealing mobster laughing and boasting about killing in cold blood an unwary police officer? Do we perhaps feel that such people, who make a mockery of innocent human life and sacred values, have forfeited their own right to be considered human, and should be crushed, like vermin? On quite another level, do we in our hearts agree with the Clint Eastwood "make my day" vision of summary justice? Do we feel a certain triumphant satisfaction when the "good guys" in a film obliterate the villains—the more violently the better—and do we think that society would be better off if it happened that way in real life as well?

There is a powerful movement today for the return or expansion of the use of the death penalty for certain crimes. Is this idea so very different, in its fundamental attitude regarding just punishment and preventative example, from the Old Testament or the Islamic idea? The difference is that the latter would consider blasphemy as evil as murder, and sexual immorality as corrupting to society as drugs, while most Westerners would separate religion and private morals from the public consensus and weal. But if one puts aside the question of *what* crimes are deserving of death, is there such a vast difference between the emotions at play in the crowd that calls for capital punishment for drug dealers and the crowd that calls for the death of a blasphemer against Islam? In both cases we find the conviction of a fundamental division: between good and decent people and those who must be destroyed because they offend against decency and goodness.

To such a conviction today's gospel stands as a challenge. Jesus does not fall into the trap set for him: he does not defy the Law which calls for the death of the evildoer. Nor does he deny the division between good and evil. But he reminds us that this division is not so easily and clearly located: "Let the man among you who has no sin be the first to cast a stone." In reminding the people of their own sinfulness, Jesus is not recommending a looser standard of judgment; he is challenging their right to judge at all. By forcing the accusers to acknowledge a basic solidarity with the accused, he implies the need of a different attitude altogether, one based on that solidarity: that is, an attitude of compassion.

The sixteenth century English preacher John Bradford, watching a group of condemned criminals being taken to execution, made the famous remark: "There, but for the grace of God, goes John Bradford." (A secularized version of the quotation figured in a popular folk song of the sixties: "There but for fortune go you or I.") A similar insight is provoked by today's gospel. Each of us must recognize that we really could stand in the place of the condemned sinner, however horrible the sin; if we do not so stand, it is by God's grace, as well as by the circumstance of good fortune, mixed in various degrees. And equally, the sinner or the criminal might be in our place: that is, the same possibilities of goodness and collaboration with grace which have triumphed in the good and decent must be present, hidden even in the heart of the most obscene evil.

If we take it for granted that people should not be put to death for apostasy or for adultery, does this mean that faith or morality mean less to us than to the Muslim or to the Pharisees? I think it means rather that we recognize that each person stands before God, and that we must stand *with* them in solidarity, not *above* them in judgment. Our task is not to eliminate them from the world, but to open up for them the same possibilities of faith or of conduct that we enjoy. Can we apply a similar principle to those crimes that endanger the public welfare in a physical way? This will depend upon the extent to which we can make our society a place that shares the hope for humanity that is implied in the message of today's gospel of mercy.

For the attitude of compassion is also one of hope: the hope for one another that we experience in God's love for ourselves. The divine forgiveness is not an amnesty for past evil which leaves the evildoer untouched, but a call to conversion: "Go, and sin no more." Our forgiveness must be of the same kind. It is not sufficient for us to walk away without punishing, like the crowd; we must, like Jesus, engage in the encounter which leads to the acceptance of forgiveness and the possibility of love.

Passion (Palm) Sunday

Is 50:4–7
Ps 22:8–9, 17–18, 19–20, 23–24
Phil 2:6–11
Mt 26:14–27:66 (A); Mk 14:1–15:47 (B);
Lk 22:14–23:56 (C)

Television viewers have recently been offered the opportunity of once more seeing Oliver Stone's 1986 film "Platoon," a drama based upon soldiers' experiences of the Vietnam war. Many will remember that this film was honored with the Academy Award for its realistic and moving portrayal of the horrors of war: not only the violent deaths of young and vital people, but also the hatred and dehumanization that affected even those who survived. The tremendous impact of the film, however, was probably not due simply to its realistic portrayal of events, but also to the fact that for those who lived through the era its images stirred in our memories other images: not of actors, but of the real soldiers and the actual Vietnamese peasants we had seen in television coverage and in news photos. The fictional drama made people think about something actual, perhaps about schoolmates or relatives or even themselves, caught in this tragic conflict. I could not avoid thinking continually of that long black marble wall in Washington with the names of thousands of fallen young men.

This film was powerful because it did not merely tell about death, but made the viewer feel for the living people who died. In this it contrasts with so many other films and TV shows in which death and violence are merely a part of a story; they are trivialized and made unreal. They become acceptable, even entertaining. "Platoon" by contrast was difficult and painful to watch; its effect was devastating. It is an example of a drama which does not entertain, but reaches into life and makes us consider its realities; it invites us to deepen or change our way of thinking, our values, our stance toward life and its great issues.

The liturgy of Holy Week also presents us with a drama. In a way different from any other season of the year the church invites us to imagine and mentally recreate the events we commemorate. But of course the passion of Jesus is for us a story: that is, its movement and content are fixed in the past; it is complete and has an ending which is already known to us. For this reason it is possible for us to relate to it in a merely "asethetic" way, contemplating the narrative and perhaps even feeling its power, but without grasping any relevance to *our* story, to our real life, which is not complete but is still under way. The passion can remain for us a narrative of objective events in the past; the palm that we receive this morning can become something in the nature of a souvenir or a good-luck charm. We can use our religion itself to avoid facing God, by occupying ourselves with the externals of the story, the ceremony, the traditional practices and feelings, and so on.

Even if we internalize the events of the passion, it is possible for us to miss the point. We can use this story as a great human and divine drama, a catharsis not only for our human feelings of the pathos of life, but even for our guilt and sinfulness. But all of this—legitimate as it is, on its own level—can leave us totally unchanged and unconverted. The story in which we take part beginning today, like every truly great drama, only has its deepest meaning if it reaches into our real lives and challenges us to face them with new insight and purpose. Specifically, the passion of Jesus calls us to remember, to care about and take a stance toward the ongoing passion of humanity: those who today are dying, who are oppressed, who suffer injustice.

The passion is over for Jesus; his story has ended in the triumph of Easter which we anticipate even as we commemorate his death. The eucharist, which recalls and makes us present to his sacrifice, can be "thanksgiving" precisely because that death was once for all, and is forever subsumed into the triumph of the resurrection. But the passion of the *whole* body of Christ is still going on; the resurrection of the total Christ, in all his members, is still in the future. We are called to remember and participate in Christ's passion so that we can also recall and participate in the passion of our brothers and sisters, and in doing so not merely recall and hope for, but also help to bring about the final resurrection.

Index of Names and Topics
(Listed by Sunday of Occurrence)